T0194966

The Spiritual Order of a Messy Church

An Anglican Perspective on Spirituality and Ministry Formation

SANTOSH K. MARRAY

WESTBOW
PRESS®
A DIVISION OF THOMAS NELSON
& ZONDERVAN

WestBow Press books may be ordered through booksellers or by contacting:

WestBow Press
A Division of Thomas Nelson & Zondervan
1663 Liberty Drive
Bloomington, IN 47403
www.westbowpress.com
1 (866) 928-1240

About the Cover:
Crucifix and altar adorn the Chapel of St. Teresa of Avila
Episcopal Carmel of Saint Teresa Monastery, Rising Sun, Maryland.

ISBN: 978-1-9736-7188-6 (sc)
ISBN: 978-1-9736-7189-3 (e)

Library of Congress Control Number: 2019911801

Print information available on the last page.

WestBow Press rev. date: 9/4/2019

Dedication

To my wife of more than forty years, Nalini "Lynn." For her love, devotion, patience, and grace. And for her indescribable generosity and dedication to the Lord Jesus, which allow me to live as a global servant for Christ. Her gentle care and ever-present, selfless, and sacrificial love ensured our children—Ingram Jeremy, and Veronica Amanda—a stable and loving home, for which I am eternally grateful.

To the Parishes of St. Philip's, Inagua (the most remote island in the Bahamas archipelago), Ss. Peter and Anne's, North Abaco Island (multipoint parish of six congregations—a combined membership of over six hundred parishioners), and St. Margaret's (program-size urban parish), Kemp Road, Nassau, Bahamas. Most of the ministry theories in the book were implemented in these parishes, and feedback and follow-up were evaluated.

To the Diocese of Seychelles, a diocese that heard the call of God and elected me its third bishop on February 19, 2005. Many of the spiritual components found in these pages were used to educate, edify, form, and shape the moral and spiritual life of the faithful during my episcopate in the diocese.

Appreciation

Sincere appreciation and gratitude are extended to the Reverend Dr. Kortright Davis, Episcopal priest, professor of theology, and formally the director of the Doctor of Ministry (D. Min) program at Howard University School of Divinity. Dr. Davis served as the author's seminary professor at Codrington Theological College, Barbados. He remains a close adviser, friend, and counselor. His helpful and invaluable assistance, suggestions, and guidance were instrumental in shaping the final manuscript.

Contents

Preface

The motivation for this book comes from over forty years of active ministry engagement in the global Anglican Communion as seminarian, parish priest, educator, bishop, pastoral and spiritual advocate, missionary, church planter, and change agent of congregations and redevelopment of congregations. This book seeks to crystallize and distill inspiration, thoughts, insights, and practical ministry experiences gained from serving more than thirty-five congregations and seven dioceses in four countries (Guyana, Bahamas, the United States of America, and Seychelles), in three provinces of the global Anglican Communion in the eastern and western hemispheres—namely, Province of the West Indies, Province of the Indian Ocean, and Province of the Episcopal Church.

However, as impressive as the aforementioned may be, my most humbling, awe-inspiring, and compelling achievement was obtained when my wife Nalini and I went on a pilgrimage to the Holy Land in September 2015. It was an awesome and exhilarating experience that was instrumental in helping me reaffirm and recommit to the very core of my faith in Jesus. It strengthened and deepened my resolve to serve Jesus as Lord and his Church as the image and substance of his life among us and for us. The numerous visible signs that pointed to Christ's humility and self-sacrifice for the world several times brought me to my knees in humble adoration and forthright contrition.

My pilgrimage to the Church of the Holy Sepulcher, the site of the crucifixion, burial, and resurrection, aroused a spirit of spiritual curiosity as I pondered the "messiness" of what transpired at that site over two thousand years ago. The Hebrew word for the Hinnom valley, the gorge beside Golgotha or the Place of the Skull, is *Gehenna*, which means "garbage dump." To lie in prostration at the very "garbage dump" below where Jesus, with outstretched arms, cried out, "Father, forgive them; for they do not know what they do" (Luke 23:34), was unbelievably and stunningly overwhelming and remarkably humbling.

The baptism of Jesus recorded in the gospels has always fascinated me in compelling and curious ways. Both my conviction and curiosity may have come from the fact that I was baptized and received my early disciplining from the Reverend Alan Jewram, the vocational deacon who served my small church, St. Agnes Anglican Church, in rural Guyana. The efficacious nature of the Sacrament of Baptism with its transformative power remains the potent and powerful influence in Christian conversion and witness. As such, a pilgrimage to the Holy Land that could include a visit to the site of our Lord's baptism would indeed be the realization of a lifelong desire. Fortunately, the pilgrimage sponsored by St. George's College in Jerusalem did include a visit to the place along the Jordan River purported to be the actual site of Jesus's baptism.

I waded into the waters of the "filthy, murky," critter-infested waters of the Jordan and renewed my baptismal vows by immersion. The thrill of that moment remains the exhilarating holy apex of my time in the Holy Land. Until that moment, I had lived my life in prayerful anticipation and hope of renewing my baptismal vows in the River Jordan. This was my life's dream as a Christian convert, someone who has committed his life to live in perpetual servitude and obedience to God. From there pilgrims in my group from the Diocese of Alabama, and four other countries, proceeded to the desert where Jesus underwent his temptations. The desert was a short distance from the site of the baptism.

It was clearly obvious from my pilgrimage that the Church throughout its history, from the cross to Pentecost and developing throughout the early church and beyond even to our time, has experienced a messy evolution. In many ways the development of the Church reflects our messy Savior hanging from a messy cross!

As I reflected, I couldn't help recalling the words of the one-hundredth Archbishop of Canterbury, Michael Ramsey. The archbishop was extremely poignant and candid in his description of the Anglican Church. In his wisdom, he saw it as clumsy and untidy, baffling neatness and logic. The church, in his opinion, wasn't sent to commend itself as "the best type of Christianity" but by its very brokenness to point to the universal Church wherein all have died. In short, the church is a messy phenomenon, a community of faith born out of a crisis, albeit a crisis of hope whose very essence resides in a "messy Christ." Bishop Michael Curry would remind the church that "because of this 'mess' we have a mission because mission is made for and from 'mess' beginning with Abraham and Sarah." However and paradoxically, what emerges from crisis is the gift of new and creative opportunities replete with possibilities for rejuvenation, revival, and renewal.

Arising from this inglorious scene and ignoble history, the perfect human manifestation of God's incarnate presence, Jesus the Christ, carried his cross to Golgotha-Gehenna. The cross was considered to be the most gruesome and fearsome instrument of human suffering of his time, and through his once-for-all sacrifice, he gracefully and authoritatively transformed the cross into the quintessential instrument of God's reconciling love for all the world without exception. Jesus continues to redeem his Church in this spirit of reconciliation. In the model and pattern of Jesus, followers of the faith are called to live as reconciled reconcilers and agents of sacrificial love and Christian service. It is my personal conviction that Christians everywhere should strive diligently to be appropriately described as "faith practitioners," in the spirit of the writer of the Letter of James: "Be doers of the word, and not merely hearers who deceive themselves" (James 1:22).

This book is inspired and undergirded by my firm and unequivocal conviction that a risen Savior is incompatible with a dying church. One of the indelible promises of Jesus was that "the gates of Hades will not prevail against it," and with Jesus, the Good Shepherd and Protector, it shall be preserved and sustained "to the end of the age" (Matthew 16:18; 28:20). Unconditional faith in the church's eternal presence in the world is in direct opposition to the fatalistic mentality promulgated and promoted by many who are predicting its untimely demise. My confidence in the Church's future is energized and validated daily by the eternal presence of the Holy Spirit in the lives of a myriad of faithful disciples who continue to give unselfish devotion and reverential commitment to the fulfillment of God's mission for the world. My hope and expectation for the continual ministry of the Church changing lives and transforming souls remains confidently secured.

The title of this book is inspired by what I witnessed and reflected on as a pilgrim, and the crystallization of many hours of study, deep spiritual thoughts, reflection, and prayer informed by many years in active ministry in some of the most challenging and resource-deficient Christian communities in the world. The content materials are informed by inspiration and learning acquired during my studies in Christian spirituality and years of experience in rural and small congregations that always felt a sense of living into the scenario of survival and scarcity, rather than abundance, affirmation, and grace.

Integral to this framework and pattern of thought is the reemphasis on empowerment of lay people pursued through an intentional and concerted strategy on formation and edification. This focus has never failed to lend energy and vitality to any process toward revitalization of lay people across the church. This is particularly true in rural and remote communities where the Anglican-Episcopal presence has existed and prospered over the centuries of the Church's presence as a powerful force for spiritual transformation and authentic ministry, the fruitfulness of years of faithful and committed work from lay and clergy leadership.

The work of congregational transformation begins in mindfulness that the people of God in their faith community are always influenced and inspired by the Spirit's presence. We should always remind ourselves that it is the authority of the Spirit that defines the church, rather than the number of people in the pews. I am in no way disregarding or downplaying the crucial place critical mass plays whenever we speak of church viability. However, in rural communities, demographics and migration are crucial factors determining or defining church viability and vitality. For those communities, it may be more reasonable to stress Christian faithfulness and commitment as major contributors in the effectiveness of ministry, and equally critical to its sense of viability.

A viable church is characterized by the conscious awareness and reminder of the early church's model. Among the virtues that distinguished the church of the Acts of the Apostles were self-sacrifice, evangelism, discipleship, faith formation, generosity of spirit, hospitality, self-emptying, fellowship, and, most of all, love for Jesus and each other. It was this defining characteristic that gave rise to the unofficial designation given to the early church believers, "Look how these Christians love each other," even to the point of willingly surrendering their lives in martyrdom. Tertullian, the Father of Latin Theology, first stated that "the blood of the martyrs is the seed of the church."

My personal definition of church viability and vitality is witnessed in the commitment and faithfulness of the congregation to Jesus Christ and love of neighbor. The illustration of the early Christians across Asia Minor was that of an emerging fellowship of few, but eager and devout faithful gathered for prayer, Bible study, breaking bread, and fellowship (Acts 2:42-47). It is crucial to acknowledge that when hearts and minds are converted, God's people will joyfully respond to mission and ministry, irrespective of the size of the congregation. Clergy and laity have wisely embraced this new way of understanding viability and vitality. Notwithstanding, the number of baptized members the work of ministry will prosper and strive. The church I have come to experience over the years works from a place of scarcity into abundance, rather than vice versa.

Additionally, it is well known that Anglican spiritual discipline and order are grounded in Benedictine Spiritual Order. The influence of Augustine, the first Archbishop of Canterbury and the founding father of Anglicanism, known as the "Apostle to the English" and founder of the English Church, was a Benedictine monk. Augustine was sent by Pope Gregory the Great in AD 595 to evangelize the people of Great Britain. As people of the Anglican ecclesia or Anglican Church, we subscribe to the tenets, worship, theology, church practices, governance, polity, and liturgical norms that have their origins in the Church of England. The Anglican presence on the eastern shore of Maryland began in 1631. It was an ecclesiastical jurisdiction of the Church of England before the American War of Independence in 1776. This juridical and ecclesiastical affiliation reigned unabated across the new world wherever the Kingdom of Great Britain was present.

With the advent of the Reformation in the sixteenth century, Anglicanism took on a radically new order, neither fully Catholic nor fully Protestant. It wisely and insightfully chose the middle way (*via media*) in its expression of Anglican identity as rooted in the catholic and apostolic faith. The Book of Common Prayer, which was developed and complied by Archbishop Thomas Cranmer in 1549 after the Reformation, became the Prayer Book of Anglicanism. Even to this day, it defines our Anglican heritage and common life in the spirit of the "bonds of affection." The Prayer Book has been revised and indigenized in most if not all provinces of the Anglican Communion, as the primary text and beliefs, core practices and principles. What are enshrined in these historic formularies of faith remain the core of our common life and the spiritual order of the church's fundamental ecclesiology, worship and order.

Churches in the worldwide Anglican Communion unequivocally subscribe to the system of belief, liturgy, practice, polity, juridical and ecclesiastical formulation commonly referred to as Anglicanism. By affiliation, members share common characteristics within the Communion, as set forth in the Report of the Lambeth Conference of Bishops in 1930, which affirms that, (a) they uphold and propagate the Catholic and Apostolic faith and order as they are generally set forth in the Book of Common Prayer as authorized in their several churches; (b) they are particular or national churches and as such promote within each of their territories a national expression of Christian faith, life, and worship; and (c) they are bound together not by a central legislative and executive authority, but mutual loyalty sustained through the common counsel of the Bishops in Conference.[1]

Prior to this statement, the conference took into account the profound diversity and peculiarity found within each diocese and province of the Communion. To solidify their emphasis on the inclusive nature of the Anglican Communion, the bishops proceeded further to describe it as follows: (a) a fellowship within the one Holy Catholic and Apostolic Church, of those duly constituted Diocese, Provinces, or Regional Churches, in communion with the see of Canterbury.[2] The general ideals of Anglicanism were also spelled out in some detail at that conference. The ideals enunciated by the bishops were the ideals of the Church of Christ, and prominent among them are: "Open Bible, Pastoral Priesthood, a common worship, a standard of conduct consistent with that worship, and fearless love of truth."[3]

---

[1] *The Lambeth Conferences (1867-1948): Reports of the 1920, 1930 and 1948 Conferences: With Selected Resolutions From the Conferences of 1867, 1878, 1897, and 1908* (Minneapolis: SPCK, 1948), 173-174.
[2] Ibid., 173.
[3] Ibid., 246.

Anglicanism then can be provisionally described as a communion that is about people, faith, and their practice and relationship to God and with one another. They are Christians of a particular persuasion.

Historic Anglicanism is accurately defined as a Prayer Book Community of faith grounded in Daily Offices and the Holy Eucharist. Over its liturgical tradition across the centuries it drew extensively from the discipline of the Benedictine Order and Rule of Life to inspire liturgical and sacramental life, including the Daily Offices. The Daily Offices remain the official lay-led worship practices in the worldwide Anglican Church.

Christ entrusted the authority of baptism to the Church, and the global Anglican Communion baptizes in obedience to the risen Lord (Matthew 28:18–20). By baptism through faith, Christians are united with Christ in his life, death, and resurrection. The affirmations in the Baptismal Covenant are components of global Anglican spiritual, missional lifestyle, and faith formation. The Baptismal Covenant affirms the faith of the people of God in a creedal confession of belief in a triune God: Father, Son, and Holy Spirit. Through affirmation, the community of faith subscribes to its call to be disciples or followers of God in Jesus through the power of the Holy Spirit.

However, the Episcopal Church's version goes a step further in including five post-creedal questions. The questions call the baptized to covenant to be apostles in the world sent out in God's mission. In the promises of the Baptismal Covenant, believers own their unique calling to be disciples and apostles of God's mission in a changing, hurting world and Church.

The author deliberately and intentionality seeks to strike a balance between grounding this work in the Baptismal Covenant, and tenets of discipleship and evangelistic paradigms in the early Church decisively proclaimed and vigorously pursued in the Acts of the Apostles, especially in Acts 2:42–47.

CHAPTER ONE

Work of the Holy Spirit and Christian Spiritual Formation

When the Spirit of truth comes, he will
guide you into all the truth.

—John 16:13

The word *theology* is easily broken down into two Greek words:
theos (God) and *logos* (word/study). Theology then is a discourse
or discussion about God. However, the term *theology* may not
necessarily be confined to Christianity, since the word can be
used to mean the study of the god or gods of any religion. The
study of religions has in more recent times shifted the concern
of theology to investigation of the beliefs or religious practices of
other religions, such as Islam, Buddhism, and Hinduism, to name
but a few. Oxford theologian John Macquarrie has defined *theology*
as "the study which, through participation in and reflection upon
a faith, seeks to express the content of this faith in the clearest
and most coherent language available."[4] The nature and scope of
Christian theology are relatively well defined: theology is reflection
upon the God whom Christians worship and adore.

---

[4] John Macquarrie, *Principles of Christian Theology* (London: SCM Press,
1977), 1.

More than that, to be a Christian is to believe that God has made it possible for us to know him by revealing himself to us. This special revelation began about four thousand years ago and was initially connected with the history of the people of Israel. This history, Christians assert, came to a climax in the life, death, and resurrection of Jesus of Nazareth, who lived in Palestine over two thousand years ago and claimed to be the Son of God.

Christians believe that God is made known to us by revelation. This means that unless he tells us about himself, we cannot know him. When asked to explain how God reveals himself to us, Christians answer that this has happened in and through his Word. The Word of God is understood in two distinct but related senses. In one sense, it denotes the texts which we have in the Bible, the sourcebook of Christian teaching. In another sense, it is applied to Jesus Christ, who is the fulfillment of the Bible's teaching and the focus of the Christian faith. The one explains and illuminates the other, and the two must be kept in balance if we are going to have any true knowledge of the God whom they both reveal.

Additionally, God's revelation of himself to us is achieved through the intentional focus of our thought processes on God through prayer, reflection, and meditation. Working this out is the special task of theology: the study of God. Theology is the intentional engagement of the whole person in the search for meaning and understanding of God. Consequently, because God is beyond our finite capacity to fully comprehend, theology becomes a discipline we not only study but, in equal measure, are called to do!

The overwhelming essence of Anglicanism is grounded in its theology of a triune God. And its theology is grounded in its spirituality of ministry rooted in the understanding and function of the Holy Spirit. Presiding Bishop of the Episcopal Church Michael Curry describes its function as loving, liberating, and life-giving.

It is the general consensus that as you continue to track the progression of mission in the global Anglican Communion, there isn't any doubt that a new spirit is blowing across this tradition. I view this as the fruit of very intentional and deliberate efforts by church leadership across the Communion. Churches are becoming very strategic and uncompromising in the investment of time, talents, and human and material resources. As they do so, they are recognizing the importance of realizing and engaging what is seen as the phenomenal work of the Spirit. In affirming this movement, there is a call for our church to reexamine, reevaluate, and (one hopes) reemphasize the invaluable contribution of the transformative role spiritual order has made throughout our church's history.

The truth is that Jesus's holiness permeates and invades every baptized Christian into the spirit and sanctification of Christ, because there is arguably only one holiness, the holiness of Jesus. When God puts the holiness of Jesus into me, I belong to a new spiritual order (Romans 6). This characteristic has not changed throughout our history, except that it has in recent times evaded the church's focus as an imperative for church growth and renewal.

Anglican spiritual order resides in the doctrine of the Trinity; God has called us into communion in Jesus Christ (1 Corinthians 1:9). This communion has been "revealed to us" by the Son as being the very divine life of God, the Trinity. What is the life revealed to us? St. John makes it clear that the communion of life in the Church participates in the communion which is the divine life itself, the life of the Trinity. This life is not a reality remote from us but one that has been "seen" and "testified to" by the apostles and their followers: "for in the communion of the Church we share in the divine life."[5] This life of the one God, Father, Son, and Holy Spirit, shapes and displays itself through the very existence and ordering of the Church.

---

[5] *The Church of the Triune God*, The Cyprus Statement of the International Commission for Anglican Orthodox Theological Dialogue, 2007, para 1–2.

There are many credible definitions offered for the phenomenon of spirituality—the work of the Holy Spirit. Clearly, spirituality conjures different meanings to different people depending on their personal or corporate experience. One clergy has defined it this way: "Spirituality is a response to God. It is seeking the vision of God and, the restoration of our being."[6] Professor Michael Downey, a Roman Catholic scholar, suggests that spirituality refers to the "deep desire of the human heart for personal integration in light of levels of reality not immediately apparent, as well as those experiences, events, and efforts which contribute to such integration."[7] He further advocates a public component to it by suggesting that Christian spirituality is, "the Christian life itself lived in and through the presence and power of the Holy Spirit; it concerns every dimension of life: mind and body, intimacy and sexuality, work and leisure, economic accountability and political responsibility, domestic life and civic duty, the rising cost of health care, and the plight of the poor and wounded both at home and abroad."[8]

However, my personal definition of the spiritual life that has nurtured and guided my experience and formation is, "being called, equipped and transformed for Christ's service." What is important is the conscientious recognition that the place of the Holy Spirit is fundamentally crucial and central in the formation process of the believer and, by extension, the witness of the Church to Christ. Postbiblical narratives clearly demonstrate that together with the Father and the Son, the Spirit is a distinct person of the Trinity. The late Pope John Paul II contended that the Holy Spirit communicates the love of God to humanity as expressed in Christ. In his analysis he viewed the Holy Spirit in the Trinitarian unity

---

[6] *The Living Church*, August 10, 1997, 12.
[7] Michael Downey, *Understanding Christian Spirituality* (New York: Paulist Press, 1997), 25.
[8] Ibid., 45.

as "the Person who brings about the communion of the human being—and of the Church—with God."[9]

The duty of Christians is to respond to the Spirit as they do to Jesus, that is, with faith. We are to believe God's words that the Spirit dwells within us and to rely fully on the Spirit for the power we need to be holy (John 15; Romans 8). Christian spirituality arises out of a deep and abiding presence in the Holy Spirit. This point was illustrated by Jesus himself when he highlighted the role of the Spirit to the disciples. Pope John Paul II pointed out that in Jesus's conversation with the disciples, "he explained how they would be able to penetrate the depths of the mystery of his person and mission only with the Spirit's help."[10] To fully understand the significance of the Holy Spirit, we must turn to John 15:26: "When the Counselor comes, whom I will send to you from the Father, the Spirit of truth who goes out from the Father, he will testify about me." In this passage the Spirit is treated as a person intimately connected with the Father and the Son; there is a divine procession. The creedal statement affirmed by the Church, enshrined in scripture, and professed by Christians clearly articulates that the Spirit came upon the church at Pentecost as promised by Jesus (John 16), as coequal with the Father and Son. The Spirit is confessed and affirmed as the third person of the Trinity. The Trinity is the completeness of God, the essence of God.

The task of the Holy Spirit is to bring the world (human beings) to the Father. The Protestant theologian Karl Barth saw the central role of the Holy Spirit to bring both individuals and the world as a whole to the reign of the Father. In his view the actuality of humanity's creation in the image of God only becomes reality

---

[9] John Paul II, *A Catechesis on the Creed - The Spirit: Giver of Life and Love*, Vol III (Boston: Pauline Books and Media, 1996), 274.
[10] Ibid, 192.

when "the Holy Spirit comes on the spot—on man's behalf."[11] In this Barth showed connection with the spirit and tenets of the Lord's Prayer, "Thy kingdom come ... on earth as it is in heaven." The attending likeness to God, in Barth's opinion, "will not be, a property of the human spirit created, but it is and remains the free work of the Creator upon the creature: a work only to be understood as grace."[12] Revelation becomes the sole attribute of the Spirit revealed to human beings by God. According to Barth's theory, "the Holy Spirit by virtue of his being present and at work is the subjective aspect when revelation occurs."[13] Spiritual discernment in the process of distinguishing between human and divine comes through human knowledge imparted by scripture and experience.[14]

The Holy Spirit is the person who sanctifies the church, that is, makes the church "holy." Likewise, the Holy Spirit also sanctifies the world. Wherever there are people working for good, both within and outside the Christian church, the Holy Spirit is present. According to Pope John Paul II, "The divine Spirit is not necessarily a light that illumines by giving knowledge and prompting prophecy, but also a force which sanctifies."[15] Holiness is intricately related to God's Spirit, which communicates holiness. By the very definition of Holy Spirit, it is "a spirit of holiness."[16] The process of sanctification informs and instills the discipline of obedience to the will of God, and the reality of God's existence is truly manifested when the individual responds to the Holy Spirit.

Christians experience spirituality as an enlightenment proceeding from the spirit of Jesus undergirded and rooted in

---

[11] Karl Barth, *The Holy Spirit and the Christian Life* (Louisville: John Knox Press, 1993), 1.

[12] Ibid, 1.

[13] Ibid.

[14] Ibid.

[15] *Catechesis on the Creed*, 172,

[16] Ibid.

the incarnation motif. Keenan Osborne sees such spirituality as "nourishment," receiving its energy from the "Spirit of Jesus."[17] It assumes a life of its own as it is given room and space to develop and inspire every possible area of the believer's life. For both the lay and ordained, it would mean recognizing distinctive changes taking place within their own states of life. It is presupposed by certain fundamental expressions, which Osborne alluded to as faith formative encounters that "center around one's belief in God, one's belief in Jesus and one's belief in the enscriptured word of God."[18]

In the New Testament, the role of the Holy Spirit is to empower. The Spirit gives strength to witness to the gospel, as poignantly illustrated on the day of Pentecost (Acts 2). Classically described in this text is a clear indication of the Spirit's ability to empower the apostles. In fact, the Acts of the Apostles is a testament to the Holy Spirit empowering the church to witness for Christ. Like the early church, the church in every era including ours is called upon to assume the responsibility for the faith in new and exciting ways by becoming witnesses to the Good News of Christ.

The Spirit is presented in the New Testament epistles as giving Christians the power to perform special roles in the community for the building up of the community. The Holy Spirit is present enabling the individual to perform well. This aspect of enabling is clearly exemplified and demonstrated in shared fellowship. The messianic mission which the faithful are called to engage in is embraced and enunciated by Jesus as a mandate to all followers who feel led by the Spirit: "The Spirit of the Lord is upon me, because he has anointed me to bring good news to the poor. He has sent me to proclaim release to the captives and recovery of sight to the blind, to let the oppressed go free, to proclaim the year of the Lord's favor" (Luke 4.18–19; cf. Isaiah 61:1–2).

---

[17] Keenan Osborne, B.O.F.M., *Ministry: Lay Ministry in the Roman Catholic Church: Its History and Theology* (New York: Paulist Press, 1993), 600.
[18] Ibid.

The Anglican and Episcopal position succinctly summarized in the catechism articulates the view that the Lord leads believers into all truth, transforming them into the likeness of Christ. The visible manifestation of transformation is illustrated in their confessing Jesus as Lord and living out their lives in love for God, neighbor, and all creation.[19] This understanding is undergirded by affirmation from English Anglican theologian Alister McGrath. In making the distinction between theology and spirituality, he characterizes theology as theory and spirituality as the practice of Christian life.[20] McGrath further posits the thesis that even in the Old Testament the Spirit was actively engaged in creation and that the term *spirit of God*, a phrase widely used in the texts, in effect signified the "presence and power of God within creation." McGrath further posits that the New Testament witnesses the Spirit's dynamic convergence in the Messiah.[21] The process of sanctification fosters the discipline of obedience to the will of God, and the reality of his (Jesus's) existence is truly manifested when the catechumenate (person undergoing formation in preparation for baptism or confirmation) responds to the Holy Spirit as demonstrated in the baptism narrative (Matthew 3; Mark 1; Luke 3). In particular, it is understood as *invocation of the Spirit*.

The visible and invisible expression of the Spirit's working in the Anglican liturgy is manifested thus: the Spirit makes the crucified and risen Christ really present to us in the Eucharistic meal, fulfilling the promise contained in the meal; the Holy Spirit is the immeasurable strength of love which makes it possible and continues to make it effective; the bond between the Eucharistic celebration and the mystery of the triune God reveals the role of the Holy Spirit as the one who makes the historical words of

---

[19] *The Book of Common Prayer and Administration of the Sacraments* ... (New York: Church Publishing Incorporated, 1979), 852. Hereafter referred to as *BCP*.
[20] Alister E. McGrath, *Christian Spirituality: An Introduction* (Oxford: Blackwell Publishing, 2003), 23, 25.
[21] Ibid., 23, 48.

Jesus present and alive; and the whole action of the Eucharist has an 'epiclesis' character because it depends upon the work of the Holy Spirit. The work of the Spirit's presence living and shaping an individual's life has transformative effects including long term ramifications for the person's spiritual growth and maturity.

The transformation within the self that occurs as the result of the presence and love of God is a lifelong process. It takes place within relationship, the relationship of self to God, to others, and to all life. Yet there are recognizable changes along the way. Those changes involve becoming more like Jesus. It is the "filling up with Christ," or "putting on the mind of Christ" experience described in St. Paul's letters (Colossians 2 and Philippians 2). It is an experience of integration of self into love. The integration involves the early process of the internalization of a beloved sense of "self," the later process of internalization of the beloved or of one's personal experience of being loved by God, an alignment with or an inversion of values that Jesus exemplified (gospel values), and changes in one's thinking, behavior, feelings, and physiology. Mystics can describe the other changes that occur within a person's soul because of God's transforming love. They often describe the process of transformation by God in terms of progressive stages: the illuminative, the purifying, and the unitive.

If one experienced the transforming effects of God's love within his or her life, what would one be thinking, doing, feeling and experiencing on a more physiological level? Such a one would become more empowered. The integration of discernment, gospel values, and total behavior occurs within the experience of a "self" in relationship. By the gift of the Holy Spirit we have been transformed. We have the invitation to become empowered by God's love and to become Christlike in all our loving relationships. God offers us this invitation in complete freedom. We also are called to invite others to learn more about and to experience this transforming love of God through our ministries within our faith communities.

Christians are commissioned by divine mandate to represent the cause of justice and promote the dignity of every human being. It is from this position that spirituality gently exerts pressure on the believer's advocacy against the structures of injustice and oppression. However, not all followers are necessarily convinced of this connection; therefore, the entry into activism should be undergirded by an enlightened spiritual mind.

All these activities, when performed in love, demand the special presence and strength of the Spirit. Additionally, in all these activities, the Spirit is working simultaneously, unifying, enlightening, and enabling us to serve God and others. Among the prominent effects of empowerment through the Spirit are confidence to witness and boldness to serve.

CHAPTER TWO

Christian Baptism: Purpose and Authority

No one can enter the kingdom of God without
being born of water and Spirit.

—John 3:5

The authority for ministry by the people of God originates
from the Spirit's compelling and redeeming work in the
historic Anglican practice of baptism entered into with Jesus
at the time of a person's baptism. The New Testament is clear
on the transformative role that baptism plays in the believers'
relationship with the Savior. Baptism becomes the matrix that
unifies the community and gives it new life. Its universality
transcends every social, cultural, physical, or geographical barrier
that separates the people of God from each other and from God.
It initiates a discipline of spirituality shared by all believers in
the oneness that is derived from this common baptism. The
sacrament of baptism can be described appropriately as a spiritual
act that may be viewed as between God and humans, connecting
the individual with God in a personal, intimate, and enduring
relationship.

The 1920 Lambeth Conference of Bishops strongly advocated
baptism to be the matrix unifying all Christian people within and
without the communion. The conference unequivocally stated:

"We acknowledge all those who believe in our Lord Jesus Christ, and have been baptized into the name of the most holy Trinity, as sharing with us membership in the universal Church of Christ, which is his Body. We believe that the Holy Spirit has called us in a very solemn and special manner to associate ourselves in penitence and prayer with all those who deplore the divisions of Christian people, and are inspired by the vision and hope of a visible unity of the whole church."[22]

Spirituality of the lay and ordained is initiated in this participation and collaboration with holiness. According to Bishop David Stancliffe, baptism inaugurates the action of transformation in the life of the believer, insofar as its anointing power is made available to believers in their movement toward discipleship. This act of outpouring of the Holy Spirit is reminiscent of Jesus's baptism in Jordan (Mark 1:10).[23] However, this begins a continual process of gradual maturation through formation in prayers, Eucharistic participation, social action affecting conversion, and transformation in grace. The far-reaching consequences of this faith act have sealed a life for the people of God that could be a unifying force for the faithful and the institutionalized Church.

Baptism's theological and relational importance to the baptized is in the relationship entered into between Jesus and humans. Baptism is the sign of new life through Jesus Christ. It unites the one baptized with Christ and with his people. The Anglican Communion's legislative instrument, one of the four instruments of historic Anglicanism, the Anglican Consultative Council made a similar statement on the Communion's position, contained in the 1996 Report. The report affirmed, "There is one ministry of

---

[22] Roger Coleman, ed., *Resolution of the Twelve Lambeth Conferences: 1867–1988* (Toronto: Anglican Book Centre, 1992), 45–46.
[23] David Stancliffe, "Baptism and Fonts" (*Ecclesiastical Law Journal* 3, no. 14, 1993), 144.

Jesus Christ in which all Christians participate by virtue of their baptism."[24]

The Church, by virtue of one baptism and one faith, is in communion with God and every baptized Christian believer across the globe. By baptism, Christians are immersed in the liberating death of Christ where their sins are buried, where the "old Adam" is crucified with Christ, and where the power of sin is broken. The baptized are no longer slaves to sin but free. Fully identified with the Christ, they are buried with him and are raised here and now to a new life in the power of the resurrection of Jesus Christ, confident that they will also ultimately be one with him in a resurrection like this (Romans 6).

The community of disciples is founded in common baptism with Jesus, with emphasis on community. A poignant claim advanced by Paul Stevens is that "those who follow Jesus and are incorporated into the family of God are servants."[25] Every Christian believer—by virtue of baptism—is invited to share in the membership and ministry of the Church. This invitation, which comes through the process of incorporation, reflects a common discipleship. The conclusive statement surmised by the Anglican Consultative Council, 1996, is "The ministry of the baptized is the fundamental ministry of the Church."[26]

There are also apostolic effects of this sacrament. Through baptism we enter into a new life and power, the power of the Holy Spirit to give the victory over sin and death (Acts 1:4; Galatians 3:27; Ephesians 2:17–18, 22). By baptism we become ministers, coworkers with Christ; we receive a ministry to be the bearers of

---

[24] James M. Rosenthal and Nicola Currie, *Being Anglican in the Third Millennium,* Anglican Consultative Council, Tenth Meeting, Panama City, Panama, 1996 (Harrisburg: Morehouse, 1996), 152.

[25] R. Paul Stevens, *The Other Six Days: Vocation, Work, and Ministry in Biblical Perspective* (Vancouver: Regent College Publishing, 1999), 139.

[26] Rosenthal and Currie, *Being Anglican in the Third Millennium*, 152.

the Good News of Jesus Christ, as we live a life of grace in the world (Romans 12:5–8; Colossians 3:12–24). It is a ministry of service to God and others. By baptism we are enabled to grow into the likeness of Christ, so that we are called to love God and others and to give ourselves for their well-being (Ephesians 2:20–22; 4:15–16).

There are certain personal effects of the sacrament. We are adopted by God as his own children. In Romans 8:14–17, Paul refers to Christians "as children" by adoption. The relationship is not a natural one but one conferred on us by God whereby we are made members of the body of Christ, as an organ or limb of Christ's living body, his real presence in the world. We are now inheritors of the kingdom of God and joint heirs with Christ so that what is true for Christ, now and in the future, is also true of all baptized. God treats us, God's adopted children, as he treats his own begotten Son. Of critical note, adopted children also have rights, privileges, and responsibilities, and these are to be promoted and lived out in the community of faith.

The Roman Catholic Church through Vatican II redefined for itself a clear departure from its earlier characterization of the theological implications of baptism. John Paul II acknowledged that the common baptism which every member within the "body of Christ" receives emphasizes their "call to holiness." The articulation of this doctrine in Catholicism further reinforces the view of baptism as the authority for Christian initiation: "The call to holiness is rooted in Baptism."[27] On a more personal and spiritual level, baptism, advanced as the sacrament of new life and resurrection, tells whose you are and gives you an identity, i.e., you are God's by adoption (Romans 6:3; Colossians 2:12). In the spirit

---

[27] John Paul II, *The Vocation and the Mission of the Lay Faithful in the Church and in the World: Christifideles Laici, Post-Synodal Apostolic Exhortation* (Washington: United States Catholic Conference, 1988), no. 16, 39–41.

of Pauline doctrine, through baptism persons are rightly grafted into the Church (Romans 11:23).[28]

The truth that Holy Baptism reveals has to do with God, God's love for us, and our relationship with God. Baptism makes us aware that God loves each and every one of us with a love that is unmerited, unconditional, and never-ending. There is nothing we humans can do or need to do to make that love available to ourselves or anyone else. However, I wish to make it crystal clear and emphasize that baptism is not necessary for a child or adult to be the subject of God's love; for God already loves us. Let me reiterate: baptism is the means by which we enter the Church and become aware of a love which we might not otherwise be able to appreciate or share with others.

The Catechism of the Episcopal/Anglican Communion stresses the Trinitarian nature of the baptismal rite by undergirding it to liturgical norms: "threefold administration of water (whether by dipping or pouring)." This is a very ancient practice of the church and is commended as testifying to the faith of the Trinity in which candidates are baptized.[29] An inward sign of grace is received. One of the spiritual implications associated with this new life of grace is the assurance of sins forgiven and eternal life through the indwelling of the Holy Spirit.[30] In addition, the baptized receives the seal of faith, the cross, with the admonition to grow in virtue and grace through prayer.[31]

Finally, baptism is more than a momentary act; it is the beginning of a lifelong pilgrimage. Baptism not only starts each individual on that pilgrimage; it also announces what they are to look like in the end. It tells them who and whose they are and challenges them to do what is necessary so that they may become

---

[28] Norman Doe, *The Legal Framework of the Church of England: A Critical Study in a Comparative Context* (Oxford: Clarendon Press, 1998), 311.

[29] Ibid., 323.

[30] "The Church in the Province of the West Indies," *The Book of Common Prayer*, 409–410.

[31] Doe, *Legal Framework*, 311.

who they already are. The church is there to provide a sign and witness for all baptized, but it is mostly there to aid the faithful in living their baptismal covenant in Christ.

It is my unequivocal conviction, derived from time spent in the church at various levels in pastoral and episcopal ministry, that when small dioceses or churches address and attach importance to their catechetical programs taking into account the profoundly significant nature of the baptismal covenant, there is greater likelihood for movement toward reformation, transformation, renewal, and empowerment.

CHAPTER THREE

The Function of Christian Spirituality

Spirituality is highly regarded as an important entry and medium that transforms followers into the holy habit of assuming greater ownership and responsibility as disciples. Spirituality as the interior function serves to provide meaning and connection in an otherwise disjointed and disoriented psychological and spiritual experience. The local environment becomes an important channel through which individuals process their spiritual encounters based on what exposure and experience is available within the diverse social and moral fabric of daily life.

A. M. Allchin points out in his contribution to Anglican spirituality that "the inner life of the Christian is evidently in no way divorced from his social and political relations with his fellow men and women."[32] Spirituality is evoked from the individual's theological interpretation of faith expressed in God and finds effective manifestation in the daily expression of that faith by the way the individual encounters the world. Consequently, this expression is demonstrated in ministry through service and interaction with other people and the environment.

Moreover, spirituality is a phenomenon that is fundamental

---

[32] A.M. Allchin, "Anglican Spirituality," in *The Study of Anglicanism*, eds. John Booty and Jonathan Knights (New York: Fortress Press, 1998), 352.

and foundational to all human beings. Michael Warren claims that "spirituality is not an exclusively Christian term. Christians in no way diminish their special attention to the presence of God in Christ by actualizing that spirituality is something they have in common with all other faiths."[33] Spirituality becomes an intimate and personal quest by those who desire to involve their lives in a more intimate relationship with God. It ultimately becomes a discipline embodied within the lifestyle of those wishing to become more intentionally involved with the gospel praxis of service to neighbor, which is the visible and public expression of their love for God. The internal transformation is a significant step in the individual's personal decision to become fully immersed within the life of incarnationally getting their hands dirty among a community of believers as an act of love and service to God.

However, we must be cognizant of Christ's initiating role in this formation. As St. Paul cautions, if we are assuming the stature of Christ (Romans 12:1f), it is a process of putting on Christ (Galatians 3:27), a solidarity in Christ, a sharing in his dying and rising.[34] Formation helps people achieve unity of life and overcome polarity. Christian spirituality, as an inevitable and quintessential constituent of formation, becomes the "ground of our meeting" with the Holy Spirit. The Spirit stands between us and the other person, making each of us mutually aware of the other's sacred value. Embedded within the spiritual transformative process is the fact that it compels the individual to look beyond self and search for God through service to fellow human beings.

---

[33] Michael Warren, *Faith, Culture and the Worshipping Community* (New York: Paulist Press, 1989), 91.

[34] Kenneth Leech, *Spirituality and Pastoral Care* (Cambridge: Cowley Publications, 1989), 5.

The Fundamental Essence of Spiritual Formation

The primary rationale of this study is to explore the accessibility of a well-formed spiritual life for sustainability and effective pastoral ministry for clergy and lay people engaged in leading and pioneering an evangelism-centered parish ministry, as rooted in Acts 2:37–47, and themes of the Baptismal Covenant as defined and accented to in *The Book of Common Prayer* of the Episcopal Church of the United States of America.[35] This exercise is not intended to focus on an exegetical study of scripture but rather on the use of texts as a source to locate church leadership within a spiritual exercise that will explore all things sacred and temporal.

The essence of leading people to God means having a personal relationship with God in Christ Jesus. In the invaluable and irrefutable wisdom of many, "You cannot teach what you do not know; you cannot be what you do not possess." The first rule of being a spiritual and pastoral leader is to learn very early in ministry the quintessential importance of renunciation and sacrifice. This rule is quite observable as a critical entry into Jesus's own life of renunciation and sacrifice (Mark 8:34–38; Philippians 2:7–8). In this vocation, our response to God must be free and voluntary, rather than something forced upon us or imposed by some external influence. It is necessary to stress the point that no one could or should be forced to live a life of renunciation and sacrifice; it is a personal decision to immerse oneself in this life of devotion and discipline. The Spirit becomes the holy influence of divine impartation, opening clergy and laity to spiritual formation that will mold them in becoming models of what Christians should be.

Spiritual formation is the medium through which Christians are trained, guided, and shaped to understand their faith, insofar as it relates to personal transformation and effective engagement in their society and the world in everyday life. This formation

---

[35] BCP, 304–305

should move us in the direction of God (*imago Dei*—the image of God). An established fact about lay and clergy formation is that it devolves from Jesus's archetype. The process of coordinated initiatives through various appropriate formation programs could significantly assist ordained and lay people to develop a deeper awareness of God.

Thomas Merton, in his book *New Seeds of Contemplation*, surmised in some way the dilemmas faced by Christians, lay and clergy alike, in the Church as they seek to exercise and execute common ministry. He opined, "Our vocation is not simply to *be*, but to work together with God in the creation of our own life, our own identity, our own destiny …. To work out our own identity in God, which the Bible calls 'working out our salvation,' is a labor that requires sacrifice and anguish, risk and many tears. It demands close attention to reality at every moment, a great fidelity to Jesus as he reveals himself, obscurely, in the mystery of each new situation."[36]

The veil shrouding the laity's underutilized call to live their lives in the priesthood of believers is replaced by knowledge, which in turn makes participants more reflective of the Lord's glory; this reflectiveness creates a place for the indwelling of the Holy Spirit. The impartation of the call to engage the divine is rooted and grounded in the baptism of every Christian. It is from this primary and formative initiation that Jesus invites the baptized to a life of shared ministry.

The church as a communion of the faithful people of God (*laos*) has at its fundamental core the community of believers, which in effect forms the heart, soul, mind, and body of the Church in temporal order. The Christian principle of incarnation is effectively demonstrated in the church when each baptized member accepts the responsibility to a "common ministry" arising

---

[36] Thomas Merton, *New Seeds of Contemplation* (New York: New Directions, 1961), 32.

out of their common baptismal commission, that is, to become involved in the world, transforming it into a community of disciples. Discipleship is based on Christ-centered devotion, which comes with an unequivocal option—the imperative to willingly give up something to follow Jesus.

Jesus's paradigm sets the stage for this pursuit. His plan for his disciples did not proceed arbitrarily; rather, the call from their different states of life was simply the beginning. Still, in reality, there was no designated period, organized program, or system theory established or implemented for formation of the apostles. Time spent with Jesus in ministry, and listening to him expound the good news, could and should be viewed as vital and consequential formation. However, it could be argued, with some level of conviction manifested in biblical witness, that the apostles' call and commission to witness were almost simultaneous. In later years, the monastic community introduced to the church the benefit of structured, orderly formation programs toward disciplined lifestyle formation. Nevertheless, in the New Testament church, the formative years were articulated in community life by two fundamental phenomena: (1) God calls all to ministry or service *"Embracing the imago Dei,"* and (2) call is precipitated by a period of formation that in effect serves to transform the baptized into effective agents, vessels, or ambassadors for God's mission and the church's ministry.

Presiding Bishop of the Episcopal Church, the Most Reverend Michael B. Curry, has earmarked Christian formation as one of the priorities of the Episcopal Church. Bishop Curry reminds the church that "Christian Formation is important because without it nothing happens." And Bill Campbell, Executive Director of Forma (an organization in the Episcopal Church that vigorously and intentionally promotes Christian formation through education), states, "When we talk of creating disciples, of moving people deeper into their life with Christ, it is the work of Christian Formation and the Holy Spirit that allows that transformation to take place."

In my estimation, Christian spiritual formation is a critical component in understanding how a person can become a well-formed, vital, and effective disciple and evangelist. Faithfulness to the task of ministry requires a deep level of nurture and formation in the art of ministry that can be sustaining and enduring, especially on those messy occasions when ministry seems to overwhelm, ready to challenge our best resolve to remain faithful, even to the point of threatening one's conviction of vocation to holy orders. We need a spiritual center that will constantly remind us that we don't engage ministry by ourselves; rather, we exercise it in collaboration with Jesus.

CHAPTER FOUR

The Nature of the Church

"… so that they may receive forgiveness of sins and a place among those who are sanctified by faith in me."

—Acts 26:18

The Anglican Church is distinguished by its creedal confession grounded in four fundamental doctrinal statements. We assent to the unequivocal belief in the one, holy, catholic, and apostolic church. This confessional doctrine has undergirded the ecclesiology of Anglicanism. The word *doctrine* comes from a Latin verb meaning "to teach."

From the earliest period of the Church's history it has insisted on the use of a creed. This characteristic distinguished the Christian from the Jewish Church, and also from pagan religions. Creed is the invention of Christianity.

The elements of the Creed used in the tradition centered round the facts of the Eternal's self-revelation. All the evidence shows that from the first, baptism in the name of Christ was accompanied by a public acknowledgement of Jesus's lordship. The first formula was "Jesus is the Son of God" or perhaps "Jesus is Lord" (Acts 8:36–37; 1 Timothy 6:12; 1 Peter 3:21; 1 John 4:15).

Candidates for baptism are ensured that they are instructed and conversant with the Creed, Nicene or Apostles' or both, as taught and professed by the Church. They are expected to understand that the Creed is the official summary of the Church's doctrines. The faithful shouldn't only be taught to profess a belief in God, but also, the kind of God in whom we believe. In the creedal confession Christians professes belief in a Trinitarian God; Father, Son, and Holy Spirit.

The tasks of the New Testament Church that commend it to the world and give credibility and authenticity to its ministry are teaching, preaching, healing, worship, fellowship, service, edification, stewardship, martyrdom, reconciliation, compassion, and liberation. Embedded throughout this work are references alluding to how they may be translated into the spiritual and ministry imperatives of the church. The goal of every congregation is to enhance long-term spiritual growth, joyful fellowship, and solemn celebration of the Eucharist in a manner that embodies Christ's eternal presence in the community of faith and by extension the world.

Servanthood is the underlying model that operates from the very fabric of Jesus's humanity and divinity. It is the paradigm that emanates from the way Jesus ordered his own ministry and fashioned his earthly life. As imitators of Christ, we are challenged and sent out every day to emulate his model allowing servanthood to be the defining characteristic that marks us as witnesses (*martyria*). The concluding dismissal in the Eucharist is a missional command to "go in peace to love and serve the world."[37]

Servanthood

It may be prudent and extremely helpful to wrestle with the question of the servant model and its ministry implications for Christian leaders, clergy and laity, in light of our calling as God's servants. It is noteworthy to recognize that one characteristic

---

[37] BCP, 366.

of the public church is that by its charismatic nature, it inspires charisms (gifts of the Spirit), which empower the community with gifts. This charismatic community by its very definition is an integral part of this complex characterization that it remains the community of the Spirit—the Spirit of God leading those willing to respond to the call to become faithful children of God. This same Spirit bestows gifts on whomsoever the Spirit wills, and these spiritual gifts are translated into practical gifts, particularly as they promote and proclaim the gospel in practical, living faith in Jesus.

God's ministers are people endowed with the Spirit to confess faith and lead others to confess God as Creator, Redeemer, and Sustainer. This confession does not exclude the confession of faith in God's Church, because the Church comes out of the bosom of God through God's personal involvement and creative character in Jesus. The marks of ministry are viewed in light of four critical acknowledgments: (1) sacrament, (2) stewardship, (3) servanthood, and (4) sign. The Church's oneness—as a reflection of God's oneness, being called out of God as to the Body of Christ—constitutes its nature as sacrament: holy and sacred.

Sacramentality of the ministry has its foundation and matrix in baptism. This is a much different recognition from some earlier understandings, where ordination was interpreted as the primary place where it is proclaimed. We are called to a level of spiritual response that is always in keeping with our capacity to respond. This finds actualization within communal spirituality where the community is open to God's many surprises and revelations that are capable of drawing ourselves and others closer to the throne of God's grace. However, this sharing takes place not only within the body, but finds efficacy in both spheres of communal life, "within and without that body." The practice of evangelism with its concentration in missionary activity, is characterized by sharing of one's faith. Every Christian is expected to be an evangelist, undergirded by proclamation. This is an activity of faith in God redeeming the prevailing fate or circumstances we find ourselves. Paul sees our fate through the lens of formation, where "suffering produces endurance, and endurance produces character" (Romans 5:3–4).

Stewardship is a mark of the faithful residing within the household of God. Accountability in every sphere of Christian life is an important rule in Christian witnessing. It anticipates that ministers of Christ follow the pattern of stewards in God's household. This understanding will interpret the ministry of stewardship to mean that there should be regular updating of gifts within the community for responsible ministry. Correlatively, the exercise should be concomitantly validated by providing the requisite opportunity for the laity to use their gifts for the common good of the order. It is in this reinforcement exercise that laity feel reaffirmed in their respective ministries.

Servanthood draws its badge from the New Testament image of the Church as the community of believers, or as the people of God informed by the words of Jesus: "The Son of Man came not to be served but to serve, and give his life as a ransom for many" (Mark 10:45). The scope of ministry is worked out at the level of imitating Jesus; we imitate Christ by serving others as Christ so served. Discerning ministry from this perspective goes beyond doing good works which incorporate service to others as our contribution to ushering in the reign of God. The main thrust of this servanthood formula finds concrete manifestation in a ministry that moves away from myopic and self-centered practices to the service of God and to the power of God's word through the gospel.

At the incarnational level, where servant ministry exists at the intersection of the human and divine, the active involvement of laity in ministry serves to bridge the gap between the sacred and secular signs of the reign of God. This particular expression of servanthood is characterized by suffering and by relinquishing every facet of human life to be controlled by the presence of Jesus's most perfect life of servanthood.

The final engagement represents ministry as a sign, testifying to the realm of God in the world of humans. As ordained and unordained ministers, leaders become the living sign of God's overarching presence through Christian activism in the spiritual and social spheres. In this way, ministry is transforming, as substantiated by Richard Bondi's interpretation that, ministry must be transforming and for that to happen, we must be continually transforming ministry .... Continual ministry is required to keep the people of God moving toward the destination of their hearts. Transforming ministry in the leadership of that movement is a difficult and threatening enterprise in an uncertain world and in the face of such wide rifts in the Body of Christ. Yet taking up that leadership as a vocation and trusting our ability in Christ to live it out is, as Paul would put it, another way of boasting not in humans, but in the Lord.[38]

Ministry has all kinds of ramifications that test the mettle of our Christian experience. Faith in the call breaks through all challenges as we answer the call of ministry to become faithful stewards. The ministry we perform is God's ministry. The quality of its administration is enhanced by faithfully and dutifully honoring these four marks sacrament, stewardship, servanthood and sign. It is the conviction that, it our most fervent and earnest duty to let these four marks of ministry strengthen our witness and, by the grace of God, increase our faith. The ordained and non-ordained are respectfully challenged to participate in this vocation of mutual and collaborative ministry.

---

[38] Richard Bondi, "Leading God's People: Ethics for the Practice of Ministry," in Serving with Power: Reviving the Spirit of Christian Ministry, Kortright Davis (New York/Mahwah: Paulist Press, 1999), 131.

Santosh K. Marray

The Pilgrim Church

> Because he himself was tested by what he suffered,
> he is able to help those who are being tested
> —Hebrews 2:18

It is an integral part of the human phenomenon even for the most confident person to display some level of fear and uncertainty when entering the place of the unknown. The Russian word *poustinia* means "desert," a place noted for its aridity but also for its ability to stimulate deep desires for inner reflection; for looking into the well of the soul; a desire to plumb the depths of the soul to discover what God might be up to and or what God might be calling or leading us into. It is well-known fact that this was a common Celtic spiritual practice embraced in spiritual pilgrimage.

One of the mysteries of our faith is the ready acknowledgment that Jesus's call to follow in his footsteps, ironic but true, comes without much clarity associated with it. I am fully aware of this motif because so much of my own vocation has been lived through this blind—or as I may be more inclined to say, reckless abandonment, grounded in obedience and self-sacrifice; this is *kenosis*. This level of trust is often undergirded by the reality of one's own personal narrative of their faith walk, that is, where God has brought them from. And yes, convinced by the constancy of faith that the God who brought us from a mighty long way isn't about to abandon us.

In *poustinia* God is found to be profoundly present and readily available, much to the surprise of those who choose to actively and intentionally journey into the unknown with Jesus. *Poustinia* works well when we exercise the discipline of recognizing whose church this is, and his invitation to us is "Come join with me, learn from me, and struggle with me, and be risen with me, reborn in spirit and truth."

The more we journey into the desert the more likely are we to get "lost" in the quest for discovery. What is dramatically poignant is that we find how much we are forced to lean on him in new ways. And we emerge from the experience with newer, fresher and clearer insights of personal identity—created for good, albeit from the natural elements of the world. The scripture reminds us to be still and know that God is God.

Recently, when I had the opportunity to experience the pilgrim's life in the Holy Land, the land of our Savior's earthly life. One discovery that I very quickly made was that pilgrim life is tough in its requirements for physical stamina, mental fortitude, and emotional stability. The qualities of perseverance and determination as well as the ability to adjust to surprises become remarkably formidable characteristics in the life of pilgrim.

As I journeyed with other pilgrims through this experience, and reflected deeply on the sacrifice of Jesus who chose to come among us, I grieved for our church, which seems to have abandoned the art and calling to be a "pilgrim church"—a "tough church," which doesn't give up or relinquish her call to be the ever-living presence of a reconciling, loving Christ in a broken and hurting world. The church should readily accept new surprises, insofar as God through grace continues to draw the marginalized, the outcasts, and the "holy other" into the sacred community of faith in fresh encounters with the Spirit. What I discovered very early in the life of a pilgrim was to accept the reality on the ground without complaint! *Poustinia*, the desert, is unforgiving, draws the best or worst out of you, and quickly separates you from the touristic mentality associated with other groups that may choose to encounter the Holy Land through the lens of sightseeing.

In the end, it's always what you bring to the table that determines personal outcomes. For my part, I wanted to experience all, even if it meant crawling on my hands and knees to kiss the star of Jesus (the holiest site in the universe, where King Jesus was born) in the Church of the Nativity, Bethlehem, or to renew my baptismal vows through full immersion in the River Jordan, or violently strike my head on the wall to the entrance of Lazarus's tomb in Bethany. Pilgrims are tough.

The pilgrim church is defined by this type of mentality, a mentality that has the capacity and discipline to transition from "What's in it for me?" to asking the overarching question, "How can my contribution make it better?" or "How may I recommit my life more devoutly to God and God's mission?" Jesus, the pilgrim Savior, is pointing us to this place, a place that draws the best from within us—that is, the place of the interior life, which is the place of transformation. The deeper life mirrors the deepening of our own relationship with God. One would hope that in truth this is the quest of every soul! *Poustinia*, the desert, may be the place God is drawing us to so that Jesus the Christ, in the power of the Spirit, may redeem his church from its self-serving attitude and fatalistic belief that the church is dying. The church may be best understood as shedding skin in order to be transformed into a more agile and healing phenomenon of a renewed vision of Christ, a vision manifesting unconditional love for all God's people, grace, mercy, compassion, and radical hospitality—a new-heaven-and-new-earth ecclesiology (Revelation 21).

Life in the exile is similar to a desert experience, with a sense of fighting for survival; a search for identity; questions about the authenticity of God's promise to God's people; a struggle with abandonment theories; a period of soul searching, learning, and transformation; and anxiety about our future as a church, and asking the crucial question as to how well the status quo has served the kingdom of God agenda.

The narrow window that Daniel looked through toward Jerusalem while in exile in Babylon mirrors the one you peered through to see, albeit dimly, that God is preparing to do a new thing, a new beginning, a new heaven and new earth, as alluded to in the Isaiah motif (Isaiah 65:8–10, 17–25).

Che Prophetic Vocation of the Church

Go ... make disciples.

—Matthew 28:19–20

The familiar refrain, "The Church is everywhere, and everywhere is the church" can be adequately proposed insofar as the Church relies on the faithful baptized community to be its voice of reason and vehicle of salvation in the world. The prophetic image of the Church derives this characterization from Jesus, the embodiment of prophetic consciousness. The fundamental role of the prophet is to reveal the will of God and establish God's reign over all others. Jesus as the prophet considered this his primary mission and set about proclaiming with authority that the kingdom of God had come (Luke 4:43). Like Jesus, the role of the prophet in community is to proclaim God's righteous indignation or anger, forgiveness, and justice and to reveal God's hope in the face of evil and hopelessness. Jesus proclaims this hope in Nazareth, where he announces the true reason for his coming into the world—to bring liberty to the captives and freedom for the oppressed: "The Spirit of the Lord is upon me, because he has anointed me to bring good news to the poor ... to let the oppressed go free" (Luke 4:16–19). He appropriates to himself the messianic proclamation of Isaiah (61:1f). As such, the prophetic church may be viewed as church beyond self, defining the essence of our Savior's atoning love for a world that in and of itself posits self-preservation as the first law of nature

Walter Brueggemann suggests that the function of the prophet constitutes a number of spiritual, moral, and social realities that strike at the very heart of human existence. In his opinion, the prophetic outreach is one of sensitivity and imagination. It connects readily with pain, hardship, and suffering and invites people to commit themselves to the pursuit of justice, peace, and compassion. The prophet also invites people to engage in history.[39] Brueggemann further contends that it is the prophet who draws connection with the past in dealing with the reality of the present and future. It is the prophet who agitates for the virtue of perseverance as a critical attribute, keeping the faith of the people from disintegrating in the face of adversity. The prophetic dimension of ministry unites people to remember the past and to dream of the future as they seek to find meaning in the present. The prophetic vision allows people to struggle with the ambiguities and tensions in life and does not seek to propose quick solutions to problems that arise. At the same time, the prophet is called to foster hope as people engage in the contradictions of life, calling them to perseverance in the midst of struggle.[40]

Like Jesus, the prophets have their roots among the people, a quality that shows integration with lay people. I keep reminding lay people in the Church that Jesus in the gospel narrative is *the quintessential, archetypical lay person* and that *their authority and permission to minister stems from his lay state.* Christians, with particular reference to the laity, are today's prophets in the world, here to bring the tenets of prophetic message to a broken world in need of hope, love, and comfort. All Christians can release this influence in any sphere of activity where they find themselves. This is how the message of the gospel with a powerful sense of Christian witness touches lives, particularly those on the periphery of the church.

Norman Pittenger helps us keep that faithful place in perspective in this landscape. He writes, "Christians in the non-ordained state have a genuine prophetic quality that shows itself in every Christian's life or work, thereby giving the individual practical opportunities of ministering."[41] The laity's interaction

---

[39] Walter Brueggemann, *The Prophetic Imagination* (Philadelphia: Fortress Press, 1978), 109–113.

[40] Ibid.

[41] Norman Pittenger, The Ministry of All Christians: A Theology of Lay Ministry (Wilton: Morehouse-Barlow Co., 1983), 48.

with the world has the added advantage of helping in the sacralization of the secular.

Indeed, if the church is to exercise a prophetic ministry, it must be genuinely involved in the affairs of the wider society. This type of involvement is an important part of an incarnational faith. Some people who emphasize the separateness of the Church from the affairs of wider society do not appreciate that this separateness from the world becomes a separateness from the truth which God has called forth from us, which is to be the conscience of society in matters of social, moral, and ethical importance. This truth telling cannot be denied by refusing involvement in the affairs of wider society, for this truth telling is what the leaders of the world need.

Similarly, the church's involvement characterizes its involvement in the human condition in a community where human need is not defined solely in terms of sickness, destitution, loneliness, or the lack of life's basic necessities. It encompasses much more than this and covers normal lives of normal people in their work, leisure, and homes. A practical approach in this representative model of ministry advocates the active involvement of Christians in improving the quality of life in any sphere and context where they are themselves engaged. This approach recognizes that the prophetic church isn't a minimalistic phenomenon. It operates from a state of abundance rather than scarcity. It celebrates its innumerable gifts, talents, and treasures and prays for boldness to proclaim the gospel in the face of adversity (Acts 4).

A more refreshing understanding of prophecy I find conducive to our modern way of life is that in its redeemed understanding, prophecy shouldn't be primarily confined to telling the future, but also living life in the present. For instance, just ponder for a moment; if the Hebrew children in the era of heightened prophecy around the seventh and eighth centuries had paid attention to Jeremiah, Isaiah, Ezekiel, and their more succinct contemporaries, they would have spared themselves much ignominy and dehumanization, not to mention embarrassment, including that of enslavement at the hands of their captors in Babylon and Assyria. This is a phenomenon modern generations need to be attentive to while exercising care to act on it very cautiously.

Ḉhe Missional Ḉhurch

The Spirit of the Lord God is upon me.

—Isaiah 61:1–11

The prophetic church not only exercises leverage in social and political and ethical conversations; the prophetic church is a missional church, with messianic ramifications arising from our Lord's own Great Commission enunciated in Matthew 28:19: "Go therefore …." This Great Commission is subsequently interpreted for substance, simplicity, accessibility, and clarity by the Anglican Communion and agreed to at both the Anglican Consultative Council (ACC) meetings of 1984 and 1990 as the Five Marks of Mission: To proclaim the Good News of the Kingdom (evangelism); to teach, baptize, and nurture new believers (discipleship); to respond to human need by loving service (diminish suffering); to seek to challenge violence, injustice, and oppression and work for peace and reconciliation (social justice) and to strive to safeguard the integrity of creation and sustain and renew the life of the earth (stewardship/care of creation).

The Anglican Communion describes mission as "sentness,"[42] in a manner and form similar to the way Jesus sent out his own disciples. In the history of God's revelatory presence, God has always initiated the sending. God may be well described as the quintessential missionary. Correlatively, God's people are

---

[42] William A. Norgren, senior ed., *Ecumenism of the Possible: Witness, Theology and the Future Church. The Riverdale Report: Presentations and Documents of the National Consultation on Ecclesiology* (Cincinnati: Forward Movement Publications, 1994), 151.

missionary people (John 17:18–21) awaiting "the life of the age to come."

Anglicans believe that all missions should be centered on Jesus Christ. We look to the life, death, and resurrection of Jesus to see how God is saving his world and calling us to respond and to join with him. Our response is not so much church-sponsored programs to increase the number of Christians or to change the world as it is to be drawn into that life, death, and resurrection of Jesus so that we become part of what God is doing. This, through the work of the Holy Spirit, then informs our direction and gives us the passion to speak and to act.

As Anglicans we are called to participate in God's mission in the world by embracing radical evangelism, loving service, and prophetic witness. As we do so in all our varied contexts, we bear witness to and follow Jesus Christ, the crucified and risen Savior. Anglican spirituality of mission sees the success of mission as determined not by measured results but by faithfulness to Christ, believing that in him God has won the victory and will overcome the world.

The Global Mission Conference in Edinburgh 1910 talked about "church and the mission," "the church of the mission," and "the mission of the church." In Anglican/Episcopal missional conversations the notion of God's mission and God having a Church to carry out that mission has become the rallying point from which all missional work derives permission and credibility. This understanding of Church is distinguished by the tremendous acknowledgment that it is a gift from God to the world.

The primary task of local Christians is to be witnesses. The church's call, according to the New Testament, is to witness. Mission is witness. The Greek *martyria* is the sum of *kerygma* (proclamation), *koinonia* (fellowship), and *diaconia* (service/ servant)—all three of which constitute important dimensions of the witness for which the church is called and sent. We read the New Testament as the testimony of witnesses equipping other witnesses for the common mission of the church. Testimony in this way becomes a demonstration, through the lives and actions of God's people, to the fact that the kingdom of God is present in the disciples of Jesus Christ. This understanding of mission as the witnessing life of the body of Christ is crucial today when in many cases mission has become a private affair with little or no accountability to the local church. This observation is worth noting since the essence of mission is in its kinetic dimension—its self-emptying, overt, engaging, and open-to-all focus.

The local church is the people of God in community in their local context. The context and church are part of the church universal; we may therefore use the term global. All missions are done in a particular setting—the context. So although there is a fundamental unity to the good news, it is shaped by the great diversity of places, times, and cultures in which we live, proclaiming and embodying it.

Anglicans of every walk of life must continually be challenged by Christ himself; all mission must flow from him and end with him. The Anglican tradition, by its very nature, must engage with the local culture and therefore take on different forms. However, the distinctive Anglican approaches to mission, which this paper has attempted to outline, are a vital contribution to our ecumenical understanding of where God is calling the Church today. Bishops bear the responsibility for guarding this inheritance and enabling it to shape our future.

The Five Marks should not lead us to think that there are only five ways of doing mission! Rather, they provide a framework from which to begin and ground all mission activities. It is unfortunate that we have taken so long to unearth this missional characteristic of the Church.

Che Mission of the Community of the Risen Christ

Therefore, we have been buried with him be baptism
into death... just as Christ was raised from the dead...
so we too might walk in newness of life.

—Romans 6:4

Those who profess to be followers of Jesus Christ are at one and the same time members of the Body of Christ, missionaries of the gospel of Christ, and witnesses to the faith and hope of the risen Christ. Because the Church is essentially the community of the risen Christ, it is also the community of the Spirit of the risen Christ and the community with the mandate from the risen Christ. Why is this emphasis on the risen Christ so critical for our understanding of the mission of Christ—the *missio Christi?* The answer is threefold.

First, the resurrection faith stands at the very center of the Christian's understanding of God and the affirmation of the Jesus Story. The God who is, is the God who became incarnate in Jesus Christ. This is a unique and distinguishing claim for us as Christians, especially as the very notion of the Divine (God's) existence has taken on a fleshly and historical form, with all the inherent characteristics of human life and historical reality. Human life emerges, it expands, and it expires. The Christian Creed confesses that the historical Jesus emerged (was born), expanded (grew), and expired (died); but death was not the end. God raised him up, we profess. That is why in the very heart of our Eucharistic moment we reaffirm our faith with the words: *Christ has died, Christ is risen, Christ will come again.* In that uniquely Christian acclamation, our faith enables us to link the past with the present and the future. We should never take those words lightly in our common and regular worship.

Second, the resurrection faith assures us of that critically significant meaning of the Real Presence of Christ in our midst. Every Christian is to be engaged in practicing the art of the presence of Christ. We are to live out the meaning of our Baptism. We are to fully activate the power and purpose of our prayers. We are to respond to the urgings of the Spirit of Christ, even sometimes in ways of which we are not fully aware. We are to gather together to worship, fellowship, and reason collectively in the name of Christ. We are to acknowledge with humility that it is only by the grace of God in Christ that we are who we are, and we do what we do in Christ's name. In these and in many other ways, the mystical presence of the risen Christ is what empowers, enlivens, and engages the Christian community in what it seeks to do, to transform, and to become in the face of a world that would prefer that the Church just faded out of existence.

To fight against this worldly desire (that the Church should get out of the way) is what has sustained the Church for two thousand years. Martyrdom and mission have always gone hand in hand to ensure that the resurrection faith was not merely preached and praised but also practiced and prolonged. So if the saying is true that the "blood of the martyrs is the seed of the Church," we must ask: Where is that blood today, and in whose veins does it flow? Martyrdom is not necessarily about dying; it is essentially about living out what we fervently believe, without any fear of dying for that faith.

Third, the resurrection faith not only inspires and reinforces the sacrificial solidarity of martyrdom, whether ancient or modern, whether historical or existential; it also gives life and meaning to the cruciality of mission. It is rooted and grounded in our basic understanding of the nature of God. The God who is, is the God who comes. The God who comes is the God who calls. The God who calls is the God who empowers. The God who empowers is the God who sends. The God who sends is the God who sustains and supports. The God who sustains is the God who receives. The God who receives is the God who sends again and again and again. Mission is not simply a divine agenda; it is more distinctly a divine function.

Nowhere is this made clearer than in the roots of our Trinitarian affirmation. God sends forth God's Spirit, not only to bring creation into being, but also to renew the face of creation. In the fullness of time, says the writer of the Letter to the Hebrews, God sends his Son. This is the crux of the resurrection faith; for in the story of the Upper Room experience, the risen Christ exercises his Trinitarian mission. He breathes on his timid and bewildered friends: "Receive the Holy Spirit." "As my Father has sent me, even so now I send you." The mission of God is the mission of Christ. The mission of Christ is the mission of the Spirit. The mission of the Spirit is the mission of the Church. The mission of the Church is its mark, its mandate, and its movement.

The centrality of the Easter message cannot be overstated either in our Christian discourse, in our Christian decision making, or more particularly in our Christian witness. It is that alone that makes us unique in our understanding of who God is, what God does, and what God expects of us. That alone empowers us to withstand all the surges of nothingness that confront us in our daily existence. That alone undergirds our reason to hope in the face of increasing hopelessness. That alone strengthens our resolve to keep on keeping on, even when the justification for doing so might appear weak and unreasonable. That alone can enlist our full and unconditional engagement in God's work of bringing human order out of chaos.

Easter faith is about transformation and renewal. Easter faith is about redemption and liberation. Easter faith is about reimagining and rebranding. Easter faith is about new meaning for life, and new movement for mission. "Go and tell all the disciples that the risen Lord has gone ahead of them into every nook and cranny of Galilee." So the disciples run with the message of Easter even if they have not been witnesses of Easter. The message is powerful enough for them to spread the word: "We have seen the Lord!" They spread it with their faith, their experiences, their skills, and their blood. That relentless spreading of the Easter message is what has brought us to this point of our human existence, our human experiences, our human expressions, and our human expectations.

As people of Easter faith, two pivotal questions persist: What does God expect from us? What do we expect from God? Just as God continues to snatch life out of the jaws of our death-making cultures and conditions, so too does God continue to demand of us that unconditional response and resolve to embrace God's mission, Christ's message, and the Spirit's movement. For as many as are led forth by the Spirit of God, they indeed are the children and missionaries of God.

Accordingly, the children of God are called "disciples." Discipleship demands intentional loyalty and radical obedience, just as much as it demands total commitment and unwavering consistency. This is particularly true for us Anglicans as Christians. May we never forget what is our identifying mark as Anglicans. We are not Anglicans who happen to be Christians. Rather, we are Christians who happen to be Anglican. As quiet as it is sometimes kept, let us never forget that the God of the Anglicans is not an Anglican! Nevertheless, as Anglicans, we are committed by our Baptism to live out the marks of our incorporation into Christ and his Church. We are sustained by the mission of Christ, and the mission of Christ provides for us our mandate.

The Redemptive Church

In whom we have redemption, the forgiveness of sins.
—Colossians 1:14

The Church is a redemptive society. By way of healing, it provides the kind of environment necessary for the release of human anxiety, conflict, confusion, and the like. It can also prevent ill health by helping people understand the workings of such things as hatred, rage, and hostility in their lives. That is, the scope of healing that the Church provides can be preventive in addition to restorative, as it promotes wholeness.

The redemptive society begins its work of healing when it

is able to listen to people and give them the opportunity to *hear themselves* or *see themselves* as they are, without condemning them. We talk, teach, admonish, preach, and pour a lot into our encounter with others. What opportunity do we give people to hear themselves? In fact, we often prevent what is inside from coming up. That is, we feel threatened, and hence we must protect ourselves; we need a defense.

The principle that people need to see themselves as they really are before they are able to commit meaningfully to God is not foreign to either Christian preaching or teaching. Yet there is an inconsistency in our approach which hinders the process of self-examination, for it can take place only in the presence of a liberator. Such liberators are those who have grown to know and accept themselves and have learned to be kind to themselves. It is ironic that we seem constantly to be passing on to others something that we ourselves have not accepted and cannot accept, because we do not know how to love our *selves*.

For the fellowship of the Church to be truly redemptive, people among us must be allowed to express their feelings without being threatened or condemned. They should be encouraged to share their feelings gently and fluently. In this way they may feel the freedom and acceptance that allows them to be themselves by realizing that no one, Christian or not, is better than themselves but that everyone has basically the same emotions, desires, and drives. Out of this knowledge they grow in two ways: they come to know, with the help of others, what behavior adversely affects them and seek to find their own solutions to the problems; and they are likely to develop the self-confidence that makes them the initiators of their own emotional and spiritual growth.

In this Christian environment people learn to accept themselves, and because they can accept their *selves*, they can accept others too. I remember the story of a father who wanted to chastise his son. The son was reluctant and came with dragging steps to his father, sometimes bending here and there, trying to gain time in his favor or procrastinate in order to avoid punishment. But the father saw himself in the son. He remembered doing the same things, and his own father had described him appearing for punishment in a way that resembled his son coming to him now.

He hugged his son and spoke lovingly to him. You can imagine his son's relief. He was pleasantly surprised by his father's acceptance of him. The point is not simply that he hugged him or that the son escaped being punished but that when the father saw himself in his son's behavior, he could accept himself to the point of loving himself. I feel sure that in such an atmosphere the son would be more willing to view himself objectively and so derive new insights into his own self in order to fashion his own growth.

Many people, when they see their deeds reflected in other people, tend to reject these behaviors by hardening themselves, becoming austere and critical in their judgments on people perpetrating those acts. Ironically, in most cases what they are speaking to is not the other's weaknesses and faults but their own; they are speaking to themselves. Much of our harshness to other people would be ended if only we could just come to love ourselves.

Is this Church ready to accept people without the slightest criticism? Or does it constantly reject itself and deny its weaknesses in its condemnation of people? Can the fellowship of the Church liberate instead of oppress? I cannot overstate how important it is for groups within the Church and for worshipping congregations to become aware that those who come among us may come seeking the release that they cannot get at their work or at home.

The prophet Ezekiel reminded the people of what I would call "the Ezekiel Principle" (Ezekiel 18:25–28): it isn't how one begins life's journey that defines them and is of eternal consequence; rather, it is where one finishes that is crucial to their salvation and relationship with God and their fellow human beings. The redemptive act that is most noteworthy comes in the journey to final consummation of a person's life on earth.

CHAPTER FIVE

Exploring Themes in the Baptismal Covenant and in Acts 2:42-47

The church, as reflected in the Acts of the Apostles, emerged soon after Christ ascended. Prior to his death and resurrection, we see how Christ lived his life while setting up a community of believers with his disciples. After the events of Holy Week and Easter in Jerusalem, we read about how Christ challenged his followers to continue the kind of life that he had modeled for them. And in the Acts of the Apostles, shortly after Christ ascended to heaven, with the assistance and inspiration of the Holy Spirit, we see the church quickly take shape, based upon the very lessons that Jesus had used to teach and inspire his followers.

In this early church, we see three great principles expressed, which were later refined by the apostolic church: (a) the knowledge of sin and of self; repentance, the change of mind, the lifting up of the mind to a higher level; (b) baptism, in the name of the Father, Son, and Holy Spirit, accompanied by the forgiveness of sins; and (c) the gift of the Spirit.

We see these basic principles emerging in the soul of the church and the hearts of its members with power. After that came the structures and the practices of the church, which still exist among us. Out of this were formed new habits, new practices, and a new teaching which first implied new learning. Of consequential significance we saw that this life was given to us as a gift to share with others. An ordained priest, whose ministry flows from the high priestly ministry of Jesus and by virtue of baptism and initiation, ordination, priestly vows, and canonical acquiescence[43] commits and seeks to respond to the call "Be holy, for I am holy" (1 Peter 1:16). Clergy, by living their own interior life with Christ, strive to enrich and define the areas of teaching they desire to give to their people. The clergy teach and minister as persons of God who have been with God and talked with God. For the spiritual leader among the faithful, the integration of spiritual formation and pastoral ministry becomes vitally important.

The exploration of the themes emerging from Acts 2:37–47 becomes a resourceful tool for spiritual enlightenment and covenantal affirmation—a phenomenon when embraced could translate into nurturing clergy and lay spirituality and (by extension) catechumens for ministry in small, fiscally challenged dioceses with limited resources.

The work addressed in the following sections seeks to offer a contribution to the debate as to how, by exploring the themes in the Baptismal Covenant, small dioceses like the Diocese of Easton could foster deeper levels of spiritual formation and transformation even when limited financial resources are at its disposal.

Christian life begins in the waters of baptism and involves the threefold profession of faith in God who is Father, Son and Holy Spirit. The version of the Baptismal Covenant used in this book is ascribed to the Episcopal Church as contained in the Book of Common Prayer (304-305, 416-417).

Celebrant: Do you believe in God the Father?

People: I believe in God, the Father almighty, creator of heaven and earth.

---

[43] BCP, 531.

Celebrant: Do you believe in Jesus Christ, the Son of God?

People: I believe in Jesus Christ, his only Son, our Lord. He was conceived by the power of the Holy Spirit and born of the Virgin Mary. He suffered under Pontius Pilate, was crucified, died, and was buried. He descended to the dead. On the third day he rose again. He ascended into heaven and is seated at the right hand of the Father. He will come again to judge the living and the dead.

Celebrant: Do you believe in God the Holy Spirit?

People: I believe in the Holy Spirit, the holy catholic Church, the communion of saints, the forgiveness of sins, the resurrection of the body, and the life everlasting.

Celebrant: Will you continue in the apostles' teaching and fellowship, in the breaking of the bread, and in the prayers?

People: I will, with God's help.

Celebrant: Will you persevere in resisting evil, and, whenever you fall into sin, repent and return to the Lord?

People: I will, with God's help.

Celebrant: Will you proclaim by word and example the Good News of God in Christ?

People: I will, with God's help.

Celebrant: Will you seek and serve Christ in all persons, loving your neighbor as yourself?

People: I will, with God's help.

Celebrant: Will you strive for justice and peace among all people, and respect the dignity of every human being?

People: I will, with God's help.

Education and Formation: Clergy and the Spirituality of the Word of God

They devoted themselves to the apostles' teaching.

—Acts 2:42

"Do you believe in God the Father?" "Do you believe in Jesus Christ, the Son of God? "Do you believe in God the Holy Spirit?" "Will you continue in the apostles' teaching?"[44]

The reference to the most holy Trinity is contained in the Apostles' Creed professed by the Anglican Church and assented to by many other faith communities. The core meaning of "believe" is an assent to a fundamental faith or belief system and offers a brief summary of the Christian faith. Candidates for baptism are required to profess their belief, that is, their trust, confidence, commitment, and obedience in the triune God. This isn't an abstract phenomenon but the living God Christians worship, profess and adore. The core of our faith is the person of Jesus Christ. We recognize that something wonderful has happened

---

[44] BCP, 304.

through Jesus's life, death, and resurrection. This remarkable event keeps revealing itself in various ways through the actions of the Holy Spirit. Among the titles scripture gives the Spirt are power, comforter, and pledge of our salvation, including life. When God created Adam, he breathed into him the breath of life, and Adam became a living being (Genesis 2:7).

Whatever a clergy member commends to the faithful—what is taught and how the material is presented—arises naturally out of that person's own spirituality. At ordination, the priest vows to be diligently attentive to Holy Scripture: "Will you be diligent in the reading and study of the Holy Scripture?"[45] The spirit and tenets of Anglicanism proclaim scripture, reason, and tradition as the fundamental belief undergirding the Communion. Although this belief was regarded as predating Richard Hooker (1554–1600), he nevertheless was credited as the classical Anglican scholar who articulated Anglicanism's authority to be influenced by a triad approach to faith. "Hooker articulated for Anglicanism its answer to the question of what is our authority. Our authority is the association of Scripture, tradition and reason."[46]

Bishop Michael Marshall, one of the great exponents of Anglicanism in the world, addresses the importance of scripture in Anglicanism in this way: "It is no accident that the Bible has a special place in the record of Anglicanism and that its language and message are so clearly stamped upon the spirituality and public worship of the Anglican church."[47] The bishop goes on to quote extensively from a very popular work by a former bishop of London, Bishop William Wand. Bishop Wand wrote, "Merely as a matter of fact, ... Anglicans ... in their public worship use the

---

[45] BCP, 532.

[46] Urban T. Holmes III, *What Is Anglicanism?* (Harrisburg: Morehouse Publishing, 1982), 11.

[47] Michael E. Marshall, *The Anglican Church Today and Tomorrow* (Wilton: Morehouse Publishing, 1982), 92.

Bible more than any other body of Christians."[48] Bishop Marshall proceeds to quote further that "this does not, unfortunately, apply to private use in the home, where in modern times members of the Free Churches have probably passed the standard set by the average Anglican. But as far as public worship is concerned there can be no doubt. Anglicans do read the Bible in church more than other Christians."[49]

There is no greater and more influential source of communal unity and integration than the Word of God as contained in scripture. This means that the clergy and the faithful alike should be exposed to greater levels of biblical understanding through different forms of biblical interaction.

I wish to reiterate that what clergy teach and how effective they are as teachers derives basically from their own interior life with Christ. The clergy's spirituality models a spirituality of the Bible that is fundamentally incarnational with transformative ramifications. It embodies our call to action as we commit ourselves to the transformation of the world. It is worth noting that, although we may express our co-creatorship by tilling the soil, casting seeds, fertilizing, and seeking the lost, we are incapable of creating the sun and water. This incarnational motif is ultimately God's, as are the harvest and its products. Let us be mindful that, whatever or however significant, laudable, and intuitive our initiative may be, we do not establish the reign of God by ourselves; ultimately it is God's doing.

The strategy of biblical spirituality has a twofold benefit: it creates the opportunity for the clergy to receive spiritual nurture, and it enables the baptized to become more responsible stewards of God's resources on earth. This in essence transforms them into facilitators of the kingdom of God. Biblical spirituality addresses the spiritual needs of all Christ's servants, even providing an

---

[48] Ibid.
[49] Ibid.

entry to transformation for people in all states and conditions of life, including the marginalized, imprisoned, sick, hungry, and disadvantaged. Every believer shares Christ's incarnation by being the human proclamation of the kingdom. And this is achieved through identifying with the cause of those society brands as derelicts and social outcasts.

Additionally, clergy teach and encourage the faithful to know themselves, and this includes knowing their own weaknesses and strengths. With this also comes the ability to understand the extent of their God-given abilities, while being cognizant of the potential and the limits of their physical, mental, and spiritual faculties (1 Timothy 4; 2 Timothy 3:10–4:5). In this exercise, the clergy help the faithful see themselves in a truer light, the light of the Holy Spirit, and through this process point out the need for the interior pilgrimage (Romans 8:26).

Similarly, clergy teach the faithful to know God, to contemplate God's glory, and to begin to realize how impossible is the task of knowing God's greatness other than in the simplest form. Clergy are also called to teach people the real nature of their Christian vocation: to become holy and to become "saints" by encouraging them to identify with the scriptural call to strive for perfection within the life of grace.

The role of scripture becomes crucial in this exercise, but it needs to be handled carefully because it has at least as many different meanings as it has different voices. All attempts toward absolutizing the biblical message should be resisted, because every effort at doing so in Anglican biblical tradition has ended up an exercise in futility. As frustrated as hermeneutical scholars and homileticians may feel, one simple fact remains at the core of the debate: biblical hermeneutics changes the meanings of texts according to the different cultural, sociological, or geographical milieu in which they happen to be read. This interpretive work, called "indwelling the text," is fundamental to the intention and purpose of the universality of scripture.

Indwelling the text becomes the key to any effective biblical exposition, regardless of the locale or ecclesial community. Passionate study of Scripture involves indwelling, that is, lingering and reflecting on a text. In the opinion of Richard Middleton and Brian Walsh, "The purpose of indwelling would be to ground faithful improvisation."[50] For Christians, the Bible is the primary source and evidence of the authority of God's word. Whatever way God is spoken of in community, this is mediated through the Bible as Lord and Savior. Terrence Fretheim and Karl F. Froehlich observed that "the Bible's unique capacity to mediate God's word of judgmental grace … can effect life and salvation for individual communities."[51]

This attention to community building is what has fashioned the heart and soul of this study, in bringing clergy and laity together for shared spiritual formation. And this is best expressed through experiencing the redemptive activity of God in Jesus Christ, the healing of wounds, and the building of bridges of reconciliation among various factions existing within the Church and the wider community. As a way forward, in a later section a more comprehensive strategy, namely *lectio divina*, will offer guidance and methodology for the effective indwelling of scripture.

Finding ways for proclamation is one of the many challenges facing all churches today. As such, opportunities for tuning in to the Word assume paramount importance. Any departure from this observation may definitely be counterproductive to the objectives of spiritual renewal and regeneration of clergy and lay, one of the defining objectives central to the focus of this book.

---

[50] Richard J. Middleton and Brian J. Walsh, *Truth Is Stranger than It Used to Be: Biblical Faith in a Postmodern Age* (Downers Grove, IL: InterVarsity, 1995), 183.
[51] Terrence E. Fretheim and Karl Fried Froehlich, *The Bible as Word of God in a Postmodern Age* (Chicago: Augsburg Fortress Press, 1998), 82.

Baptism, Renunciation, Repentance, and Return

> So those who welcomed his message were baptized.
>
> —Acts 2:41a

> "Do you desire to be baptized?" "Do you renounce Satan and all the spiritual forces of the wickedness that rebel against God ... the evil powers of this world which corrupt and destroy the creatures of God ... all sinful desires that draw you from the love of God?" "Do you turn to Jesus Christ and accept him as your savior? Do you put your whole trust in his grace and love? Do you promise to follow and obey him as your Lord?" "Will you persevere in resisting evil, and, whenever you fall into sin, repent and return to the Lord?"[52]

The theology of the quadrant principle—baptism, renunciation, repentance, and return—as proposed by the apostle Peter without reserve, prepared the convert to receive the gift of the Holy Spirit (Acts 2:38). In this proclamation Peter saw the role of the Holy Spirit in "sanctification" terms, that is, making holy the church and by extension the world. The prevailing faith conviction for mission is that wherever there are people working for good, both within and outside the Christian Church, the Holy Spirit is present (Mark 6:7; Matthew 18:20).

Earlier, chapter 3 dealt in some measure with the covenant of baptism. Its effect on the baptized allows them the spiritual gift of a new life and power and the anointing of the Holy Spirit to give them victory over sin and death (Acts 1:4; Galatians 3:27; Ephesians 2:17–18, 22).

Clearly, as Frank Allan once put it: "Ministry, of course, is not

---

[52] BCP, 301–304

contingent upon ordination. Rather, one enters ministry when one enters the waters of baptism …. Not only should we stop using the term 'ministry' and 'ordination' synonymously, but we should also begin acting in a different way."[53] It is therefore credible to advocate that God's gift of ministry is synonymous with God's call to discipleship. Christian ministry and discipleship are inseparable missional entities in the church's evangelistic life. It would make every kind of sense to vigorously promote the notion that persons of faith and not necessarily persons of power are the authentic ministers. Ministry is public activity and corporate fellowship—fulfilled within a fellowship, the community of faith, the people of God, the body of Christ. Discipleship reaches its ultimate expression in its corporate manifestation. Here, the community discovers its collective fellowship and realizes its power to serve, ever mindful of Jesus's encouraging words of assurance to the disciples: "For where two or three are gathered in my name, I am there among them" (Matthew 18:20).

The call to minister is now opened up to individual believers to be the bearers of the Good News of Jesus Christ as we live a life of grace in the world (Romans 12:5–8; Colossians 3:23–24). It is a ministry of service to God and others. The spirituality of baptism transforms and nurtures clergy and lay to grow in their likeness to Christ, to function in the spirit of love for God and others, and to give freely of themselves (Ephesians 2:20–22; 4:15–32).

Spiritual formation and spiritual direction, both of which are congruent to the spirituality of clergy and faith community, should take into account the penitential discipline embodied in faith formation. The clergy call the faithful to renunciation, repentance, and return as acts of renewal and regeneration. Spirituality is evoked from the clergy's theological interpretation of faith expressed in God, which in turn finds effective representation

---

[53] Frank Allan, "Cheating At Church," in Barbara Brown Taylor, ed., *Ministry and Mission* (Atlanta, GA: Post Horn, 1985), 74.

in the day-to-day expression of that faith through their spiritual encounter with the world. Consequently, this experience is shown in ministry through service and interaction with other people and the environment. By this constant engagement with the temporal, clergy risk exposing their own foibles and imperfections. So the practice of daily or weekly self-examination and introspection as well as frequent confession should be essential elements in their spiritual formation.

The discipline of self-examination is invaluable to the overall spiritual quest to know oneself. The use of the Liturgy of Penance is really only the outward expression of the whole posture of penitence; even after confession there is still the awareness that the confessor stands always in need of God's mercy. Hence, the liturgy of confession and absolution follows the *Kyrie*.[54] This awareness of God's mercy is always necessary to balance the interior life when clergy are exposed to the tensions that arise from the stark contrast between what they preach and who they are. The tenderness of God's mercy and the comfort of God's forgiveness are great bulwarks of stability. As the apostle Paul wrote to the Romans: "Do you not know that all of us who have been baptized into Christ Jesus were baptized into his death? Therefore we have been buried with him by baptism into death, so that, just as Christ was raised from the dead by the glory of the Father, so we too might walk in newness of life" (Romans 6:3–4). The apostle's admonition for the discipline of renewal and regeneration is important, and so also are his contemplative recommendations for every clergy member, whether in active ministry or not.

---

[54] BCP, 356.

Santosh K. Marray

Holy Eucharist

They devoted themselves ... to the breaking of bread.

—Acts 2:42

"Will you continue in ... the breaking of bread?"[55]

The Church—and so, for us, our calling to be Anglicans—is not a voluntary activity but part of what God has done and is doing in Christ. The mission of Christ and the Church is celebrated and proclaimed in the liturgy which shapes the Trinitarian faith of the people of God and empowers them for a life of ministry and mission. This is especially true of Holy Baptism and Holy Eucharist: to be baptized and to participate at the Table of the Lord is to be entrusted with Christ's one, continuing mission through the Church.

The Last Supper or Lord's Supper instituted by Jesus on the night before his crucifixion is radical hospitality and a deliberate act of divine defiance against the Passover tradition held sacred in the writings of the Torah and observed in the strictest guidelines, irrevocable and irreplaceable, in Jewish religious observance. After all, its history is rooted in the Hebrew children's deliverance out of bondage in Egypt into the Land of Promise to a life of perpetual freedom from bondage. Yahweh had acted as promised to the patriarchs, and Jews were commanded to observe this festival with unfettered loyalty, devotion, and reverence (Exodus 12:14).

Jesus, in an act with immense historical, theological, and liturgical significance, was reinterpreting this historic event based on a new commandment undergirded by love rather than law. Paul stated clearly that the law was a disciplinarian until Christ should come (Galatians 3:23–29). When he comes, he and only he will have authority to supplant it with a new and more radical message. It is one in which everyone is welcomed

---

[55] Ibid., 304.

to share in the gifts of reconciliation and God's unequivocal love for all humanity irrespective of nationality, class, creed, ethnicity, possessions, gender, and race. The Lord's Supper or Eucharist is the quintessential medium of grace initiated by Jesus, inspired by the Spirit, to a new birth epitomized through a new command: to "love everyone as I have loved you" (John 13:34; 15:12).

The life of the clergy in Anglican sacramental theology confirms their unequivocal locus or place in the Eucharistic and liturgical life of their vocation to Holy Orders: "Will you endeavor so to minister ... the sacraments of the New Covenant ...?"[56]

The characteristic that clearly distinguishes this particular expression of spirituality operates primarily within the liturgical expression of the Church and possesses redemptive quality. The Thirty-Nine Articles of Religion, which are still observed by some jurisdictions in the Anglican Communion, articulate the redemptive and hence transformative consequences of the Lord's Supper or Eucharist: "the Supper of the Lord is not only a sign of the love that Christians ought to have among themselves one to another; but rather is a Sacrament of our Redemption by Christ .... The Body of Christ is given, taken, and eaten, in the Supper, only after an heavenly and spiritual manner. And the means whereby the Body of Christ is received and eaten in the Supper, is Faith."[57]

The Eucharist is the principal act of worship in the believing community. It is the critical engagement and openness to the Holy Spirit in which the story of our faith is articulated in community through Word and Sacrament. The basic structure of Word and Sacrament is intertwined into a wonderful tapestry characterized by a high degree of creativity. In our ecclesiology it is essentially voiced through public and communal witnessing and institutionalized by human institutions and traditions operating in the ecclesia or faith community. "Public preaching is ministry and

---

[56] Ibid., 532.
[57] Ibid., 873.

liturgy (Romans 15:16)."[58] One of the characteristics of the liturgy is its corporate experience of the spirituality of the community of faith. In this regard, Edward Yarnold argues, "No one's spirituality is entirely individual. Spirituality is shaped by public worship and conversely forms and styles of public worship are conditioned by the spirituality of the worshipping community."[59]

The celebration of the Eucharist can provide a spirituality that arouses a sense of God's presence. One of the fundamental spiritualities associated with the Eucharist is its emphasis on formation and equipping for mission. The whole process of engaging the Eucharistic activity of learning, healing, upbuilding, forgiveness, reconciliation, renewal of mind, and prayer is a strengthening of the clergy and believers for their vocation beyond the walls of the Church. The Christ in us becomes the strength and sustaining power through which we do ministry, seeking to transform the world with him. This ministry, however, begins at the altar and is reflected in our reconciliatory life lived with and among others. St. John of Chrysostom affirmed the power of reconciliation as integral to the Eucharist and believed it should be shared within the fellowship. "No one can receive God's pardon and peace in the Eucharist without also becoming a person of pardon and peace. No one can take part in the Eucharist feast without becoming a person prepared to share."[60]

John Koenig, in his book *The Feast of the World's Redemption*, offers an extensive and comprehensive view of the Eucharist. Significantly, and unique in our reading, he extensively discusses the intentionality of the Lord's action and its concomitant effect on the early church's expression of it, both in practice and belief.

---

[58] Thomas Franklin O'Meara, *Theology of Ministry* (New York/Ramsey: Paulist Press, 1983), 137.

[59] Cheslyn Jones, Geoffrey Wainwright, and Edward Yarnold, eds., *The Study of Spirituality* (New York: Oxford, 1986), 39.

[60] Quoted by Oliver Clements, *The Roots of Christian Mysticism* (New York: New City Press, 1995), 119–120.

Koenig links this action of the church to a direct and specific call to mission. The missiological content of the Eucharistic meal is extensively addressed especially when placed alongside its redemptive proclamation. Ever since early church tradition, the Eucharistic meal has served to shape the identity of the church and given it its distinguishing character.

The primary intention of this reference focuses on the missiological character of the meal. This particular interest of the author has important ramifications for the church. At a time in mission and evangelism when fundamentalism is reducing mission to prosperity rather than sacrifice and suffering, these sentiments come to remind the church of its sacrificial character. The Eucharist in fundamentalist or literalist theology is proclaimed as a "meal for the righteous" or those "worthy of Christ," rather than a call to the unworthy or unrighteous for redemption and salvation. The description of Christian meal liturgies by Justin Martyr (First Apology 128) at about 150 CE was highly regarded to be the first attempt at organizing the meal in some form of liturgical order. In his account he maintains that at the Eucharistic Prayer bread and wine are changed into the body and blood of Jesus. This was passed on by the apostles in the gospels with the specific command, "Do this in remembrance of me ...."[61]

Furthermore, Koenig notes that even the authenticity of the kingdom is connected to some form of feasting (Luke 15:11–32; parable of the Prodigal Son). The communal meal setting, notes the author, had even turned out to be a controversial issue with the righteous. Specific reference is drawn to the meal Jesus had with tax collectors, sinners, and outcasts. In this episode he was vehemently accused of outrageous misconduct, to the extent of being labeled "a glutton and a drunkard, a friend of tax collectors and sinners" (Matthew 11:19).

---

[61] Koenig, John, *The Feast of the World's Redemption: Eucharist Origins and Christian Mission* (Harrisburg, PA: Trinity Press International, 2000), 3.

Koenig goes on to offer five perspectives on what Eucharistic mission might signify to the church. The five are promise, presence, practice, abundance, and co-missioning for redemption. Together, he concedes, these suggestively summarize the main thrust of the argument pertaining to Eucharistic origins. Jesus's promise not to eat or to drink of the fruit of the vine until he does so in the kingdom of God should be treated not as a vow of abstinence but as a vision of the heavenly banquet—an eschatological event consummated in the presence of the disciples. Jesus by action called to mind the prophecy of Isaiah 25:6ff; according to which "all peoples" will share in Israel's restoration on Mount Zion at a great feast. This vision to redeem the world continues to play out in the Eucharistic meals. Koenig sees something monumental taking place at the table. It is the image of the church joining Jesus's ministry for the life of the world. This in the meal becomes the agency of change.[62]

The Eucharist is an invitation to new believers, a celebration of thanksgiving for grace and the enfleshed gospel in real communities. In the author's submission, "Church growth and the Lord's Table do in fact belong together." Praise and thanksgiving are attractive in their own way. When associated with the eating and drinking, they could make for a fertile ground for evangelism. Praise and thanksgiving transform our view of the roles we play and may lead to "faithful witnessing." Through the grace received in the Eucharist we stand with Christ against all forms of idolatry, slavery, and oppression. This is redemptive theology.[63]

When read through the lives of mission, this reveals intentionality in Eucharistic theology laden with redemptive ramifications. In the opinion of Dr. Henry McAdoo, former Archbishop of Dublin, and Dr. Kenneth Stevenson, former Bishop of Portsmouth, the essence of the Eucharist is so empowering

---

[62] Ibid., 217.
[63] Ibid., 253.

and transformative that the new life mystically embodied in the sacrament brings rebirth to the believer. In effect the believer becomes the temple of the Holy Spirit, to use the Pauline description.[64] Furthermore, the pneumatic or spiritual evidence in the liturgy is strongly defended by William Forbes (1585–1634) of Aberdeen. McAdoo and Stevenson defend Forbes's interpretation of mystery as a "divine mystery" invisible to the human person, and that visibility lies in its efficacious character. They proceed to suggest that Forbes, like Jeremy Taylor, emphasized the vital role of the Holy Spirit in the Eucharistic mystery.[65] According to McAdoo and Stevenson, the mystery of Christ in the Eucharist had prompted prominent themes in writings of the church fathers and theologians.[66]

The spiritual component in practice is an undeniable embodiment in liturgical spirituality; therefore, constant interaction would keep the believer under the purview and focus of the clergy, allowing for a healthier and more coordinated spiritual formation through regular discernment of the person's spiritual progress. The Eucharist also offers a means through which the people of God can transform, through interaction and discernment, their spirituality from mere spiritual encounters to intentional discipleship.[67]

In Anglican and Roman Catholic liturgical tradition, the Holy Eucharist is given a place of inestimable prominence. In fact, in the view of Roman Catholic canonist James Coriden, its reverential attributes render it superior to all the other sacraments: "The most holy eucharist is the most august of all the sacraments; all the others are ordered to it …. [T]he eucharistic sacrifice is the

---

[64] Henry R. McAdoo and Kenneth Stevenson, *The Mystery of the Eucharist in the Anglican Tradition* (Norwich: Canterbury Press, 1997), 8.
[65] Ibid., 37.
[66] Ibid.
[67] Ibid., 6.

summit and source of all Christian worship and life."[68] It would seem to act as the fulcrum of the church's missiological pursuit: "By it the church lives and grows."[69] In contrast, Anglican liturgical theology is more conservative in its explicit pronouncement on sacramental superiority in that the Sacrament of Baptism, as the sacrament of initiation, is given 'equal status' with the Sacrament of Holy Communion. Conversely, some Anglican liturgical scholar may make a convincing argument suggesting, 'a superior status'.

However, the practice of Eucharistic celebration manifests a historic event celebrated in the life of the early church that continues to be embodied in the life of every church in every generation. Jesus identified his body broken for us with bread and blood offered for us, and every time we attend Eucharist, Mass, or Holy Communion, we celebrate this event. In the established tradition of the church, the celebrant at Holy Eucharist is ordained clergy.

The spirituality of the clergy is undergirded by this discipline to be with Christ at the holy table inviting the Holy Spirit to act upon the common elements. It is a daily necessity for spiritual life as well as for the people of God under their care. Even in the most destitute of parishes, it is possible to gather together a group of the faithful to join in the celebration to sustain the daily offering.

Although the aforementioned does articulate the Eucharistic function of the clergy already embodied in their vocational life, many clergy I have known, myself included, particularly in instances where they serve in multistation parishes, have shown a tendency to neglect the essence of "mindfulness"—that is, the intentionality attached to the liturgy—and function solely on the basis of rote, whereby the Eucharist is celebrated without the application of spiritual attentiveness. By attaching a deeper level of

---

[68] James A. Coriden, *An Introduction to Canon Law* (New York/Mahwah: Paulist Press, 1991), 121.
[69] Ibid.

solemnity and a greater degree of spiritual discipline to the action, presiding at the Eucharist becomes an opportunity for deeper spiritual formation.

Prayer

> They devoted themselves to ... the prayers.
>
> —Acts 2:42

"Will you continue in ... the prayers?"[70]

By way of an anecdote, I suppose we have all heard some form of the story of a little boy who prayed one night that something would happen. Why did he pray? He had had a geography test, and when he got home, he asked his father, "Daddy, what's the capital of the USA?" and the father said, "Washington, DC!" And he said, "Ah! Ah! I'm in trouble!" And the father asked, "Why?" His reply was, "I had a geography test today, and I put New York." So the little boy, in his prayers that night, said, "Dear God, please make New York the capital of the USA tonight so that I can have my test right tomorrow."

We may laugh at the little boy, yet there are some of us, some of our people, many Christians, who treat prayer just like that. First of all, we need to be reminded of what prayer is not. Very often we can come to a clearer understanding, especially in things dealing with God, when we spend time taking away certain things. Theology or understanding of prayer is one such thing.

First, we have to remember that prayer is not magic, and no amount of effort to pray can, by itself, begin to switch on the unswitchable. Not even God—that is, the God in whom we believe—can do that which is impossible to God's nature. So we need to first recognize this thing we call prayer as "our daily

---

[70] BCP, 304.

bread." You will recognize that this comes out of the Lord's Prayer, in which we ask God to "give us each day our daily bread" (Luke 11:3). I am saying that that prayer itself is daily bread. You must remember that it is not magic, and the very reading of our scripture will help to move us away from that idea.

I don't believe, and I hope that you don't either, that God is there to be switched on and off just to suit our circumstances. There is no doubt at all that in prayer we are expected to move away from predominant concerns for material and worldly things and instead to move toward an ever-increasing level of self-offering to God. In the final analysis, the only object of prayer is to find full communion with God. The act of prayer is always an act of seeking that full communion.

My reading of the Bible suggests to me that the true essence of prayer points us Christians or religious people in the direction of a lifelong, daily, total response to God as the one who is the center of our reality. God, as center of our lives, becomes the source of our daily existence. God is spoken of as the fountain and origin or source. We are dealing with a personal God who makes demands on us. What we are saying is that God is the ground of our daily existence. Without God, we are nothing. For us, as Christians, we are who we are because God is the life-giving source of our existence.

If God, then, is the source of our daily existence, and if, as I have just shared, true prayer has to do with total response, then it seems to me, and I hope to you, too, that prayer has to be for us our daily bread. Real bread is that without which no hope of nurture can be sustained. If prayer, then, has to be the means whereby we are able to recollect and appropriate as far as we can that abiding sense of the presence of God in the world and in our lives, it seems to me that in our lives as Christians, who claim to have a personal relationship with this God, we must seek to govern and conduct ourselves within that frame of reference.

It has been said that Anglicans cannot pray without the book.

But let it also be said that when we pray with the book, we say it well. We read our prayers with meaning, and they don't go dry on us. Although they are coming from the book, we are filling them with meaning. We don't have to apologize to anyone for that. The fact is that we are always using the moment, and prayer has to do most with that moment, rather than with the form, whether from the book or not. Above all, prayer must mean something if we are treating it as important. Here, again, the Bible gives a wonderful demonstration of how more and more prayer moves away from complaining and begging to become words of adoration, thanksgiving, and praise.

Biblical prayer takes the confessor seriously. I think that without the serious acknowledgment of our unworthiness before God, we will not be able to enjoy the fruits of contemplation. Contemplation in the majestic presence of one who is called a loving creator, a loving redeemer, and a loving persuader. We find that so much of our prayers jump from thanksgiving to begging. You should not go up to lead worship in ministry without expressing a sense of unworthiness even to be in God's presence. You may find that sometimes it works and sometimes it doesn't. We go back, of course, to that good old Anglican form in the acronym PACTS—Preparation (Pause), Adoration, Confession, Thanksgiving, and Supplication. The psalmist reminds us to just "be still, and know that I am God!" (Psalm 46:10); that is, to keep quiet first. So I make good of this need for a sense of unworthiness before God.

I point now to Psalm 51, a tremendous psalm that focuses on the contrite heart: "Create in me a clean heart, O God, and put a new and right spirit within me" (Psalm 51:10). This helps us understand why even one phrase for the words *to pray* means to "draw near." Praying to God means drawing near to God. And those who draw near to the holy God are always conscious of their own unworthiness and therefore find it impossible to address God without acknowledging the stark reality of this fact.

Daily, however, we are forced to recognize that in spite of this majestic holiness of God, we are also upheld and strengthened by God's redeeming mercy. It is only through this mercy that we are able to carry on—not only with the business of prayer itself, but also with the business of living in this world that would rather not hear God's name at all except in blasphemy. Prayer in such daily situations of life becomes like manna from heaven; it becomes a daily feeding, a daily mixture, because so many think they can do without it and they care not to live it. One of the central issues in Christian spirituality is to see how ultimate reality becomes intimate reality. This must never escape us, because we can be overwhelmed by a sense of God's all-inspiring majesty and the feeling that since God is so far away, we can move away; the feeling that because we can't get there, we should just leave it alone and move in the other direction.

If prayer as daily bread is response and communion and seeking the church for communion with God, if it is addressed to God that we are trying to approach the throne of grace in spite of our unworthiness, let us also go on to say that prayer is also our availability for God. That is, making ourselves available for God. For this availability is not of our own making or decision. We dare not forget that prayer itself ultimately depends not on our own initiative but on God's initiative. Whenever we choose to pray, it is only because God has already made that choice possible. It is not the place that matters, it is the fact that you can spend the time anywhere, but it is always to be chosen by God.

To choose God is always, in fact, to have been chosen by God. This means that our daily prayers are constant reminders that we are chosen daily by God to be God's chosen. We recall what Jesus said to his friends, "You did not choose me but I chose you. And I appointed you to go and bear fruit" (John 15:16).

A critical scripture verse is found in the First Letter of John: "We love because he first loved us" (1 John 4:19). I want you to know that this text is often misrepresented for people who are beginning to become a little too spiritually arrogant about their sense of holiness and religious sense of excellence. A healthy caution, at no step of the way can we ever be so presumptuous as to take credit for knowing a little more about God than others do, as having a hotline to God that they don't have, or having a revelation from God that is hidden from others. You can never switch on God; it is always true that God has taken the initiative. I believe that it is through the work of God, the Holy Spirit, that we ourselves are enabled to offer to God what is pleasing in God's sight.

One school of thought suggests that God is hard to please. Maybe they are correct. But it seems to me that, from the spiritual point of view, the fact that we are making ourselves available to God is always a good thing, and it has some merit to it. Very often in our prayers we have difficulty with not just sleeping, but wandering and disturbing thoughts, and it bothers us a great deal. You caught yourself and went back. After all, they must be pleasing because, in the final analysis, we are creatures, and God, who is the Creator, understands that creatures are made that way, and they will go off in that direction. God, having created us, makes allowance for these things in our lives. The fact that we aim to go toward God says to me to that we certainly are worthy of him.

What does this mean? It means that in this spirit of availability we should seek to make our whole selves available—not partially available but wholly available. By that I mean everything about us: our sounds, our voices, our feelings, our breathings, our relationships (even with other Christians or those who have no faith at all), our jobs, our children, our communities. I am saying that our understanding of prayer must be so comprehensive and so integrated that we do not separate some sections of our lives as compartments where God and our relationships with God must not interfere. Availability, therefore, involves the totality of ourselves.

Is this all that prayer involves? Are there other dimensions to be taken into account? Communion, address, response, and availability? Yes, there are others. Let me briefly share some with you:

Santosh K. Marray

Yielding

Let us look, for example, at prayer as a yielding. The words *surrender* and *submission* can be used instead. Yielding, for the Christian, is sometimes difficult because all of us are quite often overcome by our own sense of self-importance. Other things bother us as well—the cares of the world, the preoccupation of getting things done right, the agreements that we make (we have given our word, so we have to keep it), the anxiety that bothers us, and the kind of restlessness that we have and get from living in a restless world beset by all kinds of human feelings. We are surrounded by them, and because of this we don't seem to have any time to yield anything of ourselves up to God. Prayer means bending our will toward God in spite of everything; it means opening up every department of our existence to God so that we can honestly say, with young Samuel, "Speak, for your servant is listening" (1 Samuel 3:10b). Or take Saul of Tarsus, who realized that he couldn't go any further, and the voice came, saying, "Saul, Saul, why do you persecute me? It hurts you to kick against the goads" (Acts 9:4; 26:14). His response was, "What am I to do, Lord?" (Acts 22:10). He gave himself over to an extremely different life. Therefore, yielding is an essential form of our prayer.

Clarity

Sometimes our prayers are so confusing that even we have difficulty understanding what we are praying about. Prayer is for our own identification. One of the great things about having the prayer book is that it helps to get rid of a lot of the "floweriness" unleashed on a congregation.

Prayer requires a growing clarity—a clarity not of what is said, but about the one who is saying it. It must always be growing clearer and clearer. And we have to go beyond our limitations and cut through all the fuzziness of our mood and simply allow God to see us and hear us as we really are (recognizing that he already does). We need to be aware that our words in prayer may hide the true state of our heart, because sometimes we really don't mean what we say. We may make promises, verbal commitments to God that we have no intention of fulfilling. We look at the outward appearance, but God looks and listens to the heart. This was how God put it to the prophet Samuel at the anointing of young David as king (1 Samuel 16:7). This, in effect, is what I mean by clarity of prayer.

Prayer as Fellowship

True prayer always leads to stronger fellowship with those with whom we pray. It also leads to better fellowship with those for whom we pray. True prayer breeds bonds of love with others. It produces a higher as well as a deeper level of friendship in God. This is not found just by seeking friendship but by seeking God. Through genuine prayer, our friendships are purified and bound up by faith and that common reference for God.

How is it possible for us to be praying for one another daily, praying with others weekly, and not have any sense of fellowship and friendship in God? It doesn't seem to go together. I honestly believe, then, that genuine prayer creates an authentic friendship in God, and those friendships that are not authentic can be purified as well.

Three Ways of Prayer

If prayer is to become our daily bread, then we have to allow prayer to pass through us in the three basic ways of spiritual growth. They are

1. the purgative way: This is the means by which we gradually experience a change of heart and mind;
2. the illuminative way: This is the way through which not only do we discover who we really are, but more and more

we are enlightened by the grace of God, enlightened by God's will; and

3. the unitive way: This is the means by which we realize a deeper sense of communion with God in every aspect of our being.

It is here in this unitive way that we often realize that God is not necessarily moved by sweet-sounding words of praise. Often it is during the moment of silence in our lives that we speak the loudest and strongest in God's presence.

When all is said and done, always remember that no prayer can exceed the prayer that God has provided for us in Jesus Christ—not by Jesus Christ, but in Jesus Christ. For each Christian heart, to pray in Christ is to pray with Jesus.

As the apostle Paul reminds us, "it is no longer I who live, but it is Christ who lives in me" (Galatians 2:20). He is living in me, he is praying in me, and he is that constant daily prayer because he intercedes for us in heavenly places. As the writer to the Hebrews reminds us, "he always lives to make intercession for them" (Hebrews 7:25).

Yet each one of us has our own mountains and valleys, good days and dark nights. In spite of the problems and events that surround us, we are concerned with each other's tragedies and share in each other's pain. We still, in spite of our pain, provide many possibilities for embracing that promise of wholeness and freedom won for us in Christ. As bad as the world is out there, in the context of harsh, unclean, and evil manifestations, still, as God's servants especially called by God, we are summoned daily to God's temple to be filled again with that majestic holiness with which the prophet Isaiah, in chapter 6 of his prophecy, was so profoundly inspired in the temple.

It is St. Paul who makes it easy for us. "Do you not know that your body is a temple of the Holy Spirit within you, which you have from God, and that you are not your own?" (1 Corinthians

6:19). Therefore, let us see, as we daily feed on the presence of God, whether we can experience a transformation in which that presence can lead to confession, confession can lead to cleansing, cleansing can lead to some commitment, and that commitment can lead to commission. As Christians we live daily prayer in the spirit of contrition, confession, and conversion. The whole point of being committed to God's way is that God is always converting us in order to keep sending us on. For when God feeds us with the daily bread, we are fed not so much to be fatter, but to be stronger in grace, faith, and holiness for the process of living.

We are equipped and commissioned for ministry and to service. Our response to God's daily feeding isn't "Thank you, Lord," and expecting some more tomorrow; rather, it is always to be what Isaiah says, "Here am I; send me!" (Isaiah 6:8b).

Clergy are highly regarded as persons of prayer; therefore, the integrity of their spiritual formation is sustained by familiarity with prayer, its byways, its delights, and its difficulties. From that familiarity they teach; from their failures they warn; and from progress they encourage. The clergy member is the person of God who has set time to pray and to be with God as an absolute priority. To be more precise, the clergy is determined to receive "daily bread." This is the mixture of prayer, Eucharist, meditation, and quietness. In these occupations, clergy, as did Moses, will speak with God face to face, and their people will know that they have been with God (Exodus 33:11; 34:30; cf. 2 Corinthians 3:7).

As a matter of spiritual discipline, in the ordinal of ordination, clergy covenanted by vow to live a life of prayer, whether conforming to the ancient practice of the Divine Office or any form of daily discipline appealing to them. It is one of their primary religious obligations; but the way they say it, their attitude and intentions, will also be significant. The Office is there to feed, sustain, and nourish interiorly. It can also serve as an excellent vehicle for priestly work of intercession. In the opinion of Robert Benson, the Office has communal consequences and is undergirded by the history of the church in its ability to draw the clergy into reflection. He states that in his view, "Praying the daily office connects us to the whole community of Christ for all time past and for all time to come. It anchors us in the ongoing of the church itself, requiring us to maintain the cascade of the prayer of the faithful, the Work of God itself."[71]

Many clergy weave into their Offices the names of the baptized, the confirmed, the sick, the needy, and so on, offering the various sections of the Office for them. They let "the cycle of prayer that comes and goes each day and week and month keep calling others to mind: those who are lost, and those who are ill, those who are alone, and those who are at war, those who are afraid and those who have no home."[72] There is a sense of newness to the day that comes through engaging God. The Office "frames the day with praise and thanksgiving and service; it serves to make the worship of God the center of our life and changes the focus of our prayers from the created to the Creator."[73] It goes without saying that the Office is also a fruitful source of material to enrich meditation.

The spiritual benefits derived from the Office should also enhance the prayer habit of the laity with equal outcomes. In ministry in certain parts of the Anglican Communion, as clergy in charge of several congregations, I have had to utilize the services of lay leaders as Lay Readers and Catechists. Training in the Daily Office was a necessary component of their training, because it was the Order of Service they were canonically and liturgically permitted to conduct. This translated to the majority of members becoming familiar with the use of the Daily Office and practicing it as a daily spiritual discipline.

My reading of the Bible suggests that the true essence of

---

[71] Robert Benson, *A Good Life: Benedict's Guide to Everyday Joy* (Brewster, MA: Paraclete Press, 2004), 23.

[72] Ibid.

[73] Ibid.

prayer points lay and clergy alike in the direction of a lifelong and total response to God as the one who is the center of our reality (Matthew 21:22; 1 Corinthians 7:5; Philippians 4:6–7; 1 Peter 3:7, 12). God, as the center of our lives, becomes the source of our daily existence (1 Timothy 6:17). The psalmist writes, "He provides food for those who fear him" (Psalm 111:5). God is spoken of as the fountain and origin or source. What I am recognizing is that God is the cause of our daily existence. Without God, we are nothing. For us, as Christians, we are who we are because God is the life-giving source of our existence.

Prayer also means bending our will toward God, in spite of everything; it means opening up every department of our existence to God so that we can honestly say with young Samuel, "Speak, for your servant is listening" (1 Samuel 3:10).

Pastoral and Spiritual Care

They devoted themselves to ... fellowship.

—Acts 2:42

"Will you continue in ... fellowship?"[74]

Pastoral care is a revered expression of the church's mission and has shaped the church's witness over the centuries in the life of the Good Shepherd. As the faith of the church continues to spread, it is imperative that clergy become involved with people in their real circumstances of daily life. The spirituality of clergy must come to terms with the liberating influence of this type of ministry and its potential to have inestimable effects on the mission of the church.

Clergy should be mindful of the intrinsic value of pastoral care to the community of faith. Robert Kinast succinctly points out, "Pastoral care has a venerable image in Christian history. It

---

[74] BCP, 304.

is rooted in biblical references which express the attitude, motive, and style of ministry right up to our own day."[75]

Spiritual direction is connected to the role of spiritual director, who is someone trained and knowledgeable in the discipline and sensibility of spiritual direction. They may be invited to be someone with whom parishioners may test where they may be on their spiritual journey. Urban T. Holmes describes a spiritual director as "a kind of navigational fix—someone with whom we can find solace in times of great stress, check out personal decisions, tap for new ideas or directions, and make our confession."[76]

Pastoral care and spiritual direction have their fundamental origin in God, who was the first caregiver and continues to exercise that ministry. As God's chosen vessels and agents, clergy are called to exercise their mission in the life of others and, where possible, educate the laity to do likewise as a model of Jesus to his disciples. Within the setting of spiritual formation, clergy as caregivers and spiritual directors function as a critical link between believers and God as they attempt to sort through the many idiosyncrasies and innuendoes involved in spiritual formation.

Jennifer A. Bakke succinctly reminds us that the faithfulness of God is at the core of spiritual direction. When we seek spiritual direction, we are utterly dependent on God and God's love reaching for us …. We need encouragement to trust God to be God, to trust the Holy Spirit in another person, and to trust God for a particular spiritual direction relationship. It is helpful to remember that all the initiative is not ours. In fact, any movement on our part toward God is an indicator that God has been seeking us.[77]

As such, clergy trained in the art of spiritual direction offer

---

[75] Robert L. Kinast, *Caring for Society: A Theological Interpretation of Lay Ministry* (Chicago: The Thomas More Press, 1985), 96.

[76] Urban T. Holmes III, *Spirituality for Ministry* (Harrisburg, PA: Morehouse Publishing, 2002), 171.

[77] Jeanette A. Bakke, *Holy Invitations: Exploring Spiritual Direction* (Grand Rapids: Baker Books, 2000), 21.

invaluable assistance as pastoral counselors in this particular blend of spirituality in terms of spiritual friendship and companionship. However, they must exercise caution to attentively assess when the needs of the individual have arisen to a point that may require professional assistance from a qualified spiritual director.

In spiritual formation, the clergy understand that pastoral care is an investment to love what they do in service of others. The concept of *koinonia* or *Christian fellowship* or *unity* is the acknowledgment that we are all one body in Christ. The church depends on the health, well-being, and vitality of its membership to express that unity, and here more than anywhere else, the clergy role as spiritual director comes in.

The heightened awareness that God is generally viewed as elusive requires constant discernment. This invariably lies at the heart of the spiritual director. Kenneth Leech articulates the spiritual director's role as pointing the believer to a sense of discernment when he states, "The spiritual director is concerned with the attainment of spiritual discernment."[78] Bakke points out that in essence, "when we seek God, we discover that God is trustworthy in ways that are far beyond anything we have imagined. Scripture assures us that God does respond, that God hears, cares, and answers."[79]

Spiritual discernment is the divine and spiritual gift to be able to recognize that the faithful cannot be taken for granted and that their complexities should be respected. Each individual has to be cared for in their unique and peculiar circumstances of life. We see this principle activated and employed in the post-Pentecost selection of the seven deacons (Acts 6). In this paradigm, the quality of measurement applied was that care was offered after careful consideration of the circumstances of need, using that as a guide to the appropriate response as discerned by the early apostles.

---

[78] Leech, *Spirituality and Pastoral Care*, 70.

[79] Bakke, *Holy Invitations*, 22.

Clergy spirituality, administered in pastoral care and spiritual direction, serves to transform clergy into living agents of God's love as shown in Jesus and lived out in the early church. The gravity of the imperative for clergy to actively pursue the art of spiritual direction is summed up by Kenneth Leech in this way: "The picture I see is of society in which more and more people are looking for a sense of spiritual direction, and the problem for clergy and others is how to meet that need adequately without being overwhelmed."[80]

Leech indicates his personal agreement with Martin Thornton that "spiritual direction is our greatest pastoral need today."[81] How true is the adage from my former Bishop of the Bahamas, the late Michael H. Eldon, who was known to remind his clergy that "a home-going priest makes a churchgoing people!" In his unique episcopal care for his clergy, he was calling to our minds the critical role pastoral care plays in the effective exercising of our ministry. Certainly, in such a pastoral context, clergy who minister in this strategy embody phenomenal pastoral transformation that in time has translated into profound church growth and stability.

Ecumenical/Interfaith Relations

All who believed were together and had all things in common.
—Acts 2:44

"Will you continue in ... fellowship?"[82]

The Church community has a responsibility to foster external interaction or risk the danger of developing internal exclusivism. The action of the early church manifests a church in fellowship

---

[80] Kenneth Leech, *Soul Friend: An Invitation to Spiritual Direction* (New York: HarperCollins Publishers, 1992), 2.

[81] Ibid.

[82] BCP, 304.

inspired by the Spirit, which produced *koinonia* or fellowship. It is the overwhelming conviction of many persons of faith that the real essence of Pentecost lies in the assemblage of diverse people "from every nation under heaven living in Jerusalem" (Act 2:5) to form a unified body of believers.[83] In the opinion of William H. Willimon, this action in no way describes a momentary, selfless spontaneity; rather, for him it expresses a spirituality of freedom. "Everything they once held has been set free so that the word *koinonia* means something."[84] All are one body in God through Christ in the pervading work of the Holy Spirit.

The spirituality of the clergy points them to an outward-looking Church, an institution that functions beyond denominational boundaries to incorporate the fundamental spirituality embodied in *koinonia*. It is the fellowship of feeling, life, thought, and word: people knowing each other not through mere earthly ties but because they are in God and God is in them. This feeling leads on to communion and partakes in the joy and faith of those who share common core values of faith, namely the incarnation, resurrection, and atonement, the Trinity, and the authority of the Bible. The early church continued in daily communion prompted by the heart's need and hunger; they continued in daily prayer; asking for all that the company of believers needed.

The first converts were baptized and received the gift of the Holy Spirit, and we find that the church grew at once, meeting in the temple and breaking bread from house to house. Christian spirituality embraces the outer expression of these principles within; when they communicate such spiritual habits, the faithful are sure to emulate the holy habits of Christian life.

The ecumenical spirit in historic Anglicanism has been vigorously attested to in many documents and councils and further

---

[83] William H. Willimon, *Acts Interpretation: A Bible Commentary for Teaching and Preaching* (Atlanta: John Knox Press, 1988), 40.
[84] Ibid., 40–41.

undergirded and recognized in the 1996 Report of the Anglican Consultative Council that "there is one ministry of Jesus Christ in which all Christians participate by virtue of their baptism."[85] The Church as communion, by virtue of one baptism and one faith, is in communion with God and every baptized Christian believer across the globe. Jesus in the high priestly prayer agonizes for the unity of the church: "that they may be one, as we are one, I in them and you in me, that they may become completely one" (John 17:22–23).

This admonition arises out of a recognition that the spirituality of the Anglican Communion places particular emphasis on the holy Trinity in which Father, Son, and Holy Spirit are both distinct in expression yet united in function. Within the context of this doctrine, the communion sees ministry of the whole body and holds firm in its attestation that the Church is the body of Christ. As a result, deliberate efforts should be made to encourage all to participate by sharing their distinctive gifts, ministries, cultures, and other qualities. To achieve this goal, "the Church discerns and identifies all discriminatory practices in its structure, images and symbols, and commits itself to reform and renewal."[86]

The apostle Paul's metaphor of the church as the body of Christ is a biblical foundation for an ecumenical approach to Christian spirituality. In Ephesians 4:1ff., Paul articulates the theme of the one body and its many members according to varied gifts and speaks also of the spiritual dispositions associated with unity and maturity in Christ.

In this reference, it is believed that the apostle is commenting on the unity within the local church, with gifts of members differing according to various functions or emerging orders for ministry. This passage from Ephesians calls for a celebration of

---

[85] Rosenthal and Currie, *Being Anglican in the Third Millennium*, 152.
[86] Ibid., 191.

such ecclesial gifts within the spiritual parameter, noting with a degree of clarity each person's maturity (full stature) in Christ. And with particular emphasis in addressing the healthy, well-equipped body of Christ, these characteristics are nurtured in healthy ways: humility, gentleness, patience, bearing with one another in love, speaking the truth in love, unity of faith, the bond of peace, and knowledge of the Son of God.

In 1 Corinthians 12:12ff, Paul elaborates on the body of Christ metaphor, establishing a sense of the unity in diversity of the body and the indebtedness of each member of the body to all others. Christian spirituality, as the practice of the faith in its maturity, has an ecumenical quality that honors other members of the body and other ecclesial traditions, even when they are considered inferior, broken, or incomplete. Christian spirituality does not know its fullness until all expressions of the members of the body are honored. The clergy, in the role of spiritual director(s) in the congregation, see ecumenical events as being integral to their spirituality. In my former Diocese of Seychelles it was common for the ecumenical movement to witness through the Week of Prayer for Christian Unity, Women's World Day of Prayer, annual opening of the Supreme Court, social outreach, and issuance of joint proclamations on special occasions in national life.

The fostering of joint Christian witness and discipleship is an inescapable message and mandate of Jesus. The apostle John recalls for us in the High Priestly prayer the central vision of Jesus for the church and by extension the world, "for all to be one so that the whole be one" (John 17). Any spirituality that the priests choose to engage and eventually make their own must take seriously this commission. The words of the psalmist provide fertile ground for this ecclesiology: "Oh, how good and pleasant it is, when brethren live together in unity!" (Psalm 133:1). The ecumenical role of clergy is very important in the overall scheme of Christian leadership, discipleship, and spiritual formation.

Witness and Evangelism

Many wonders and signs were being done by the apostles.

—Acts 2:43

And that day about three thousand persons were added.

—Acts 2:41

And day by day the Lord added to their
number those who were being saved.

—Acts 2:47

"Will you proclaim by word and example the
Good News of God in Christ?"[87]

On this theme, I advocate making a case for reclaiming one of the fundamental mandates of Jesus to his church: "to proclaim the good news of the kingdom"; the command to "go … make disciples." I wish to do so by advocating for the redemption of the word *evangelism* and its reintroduction into the fabric of the everyday vocabulary of the Episcopal Diocese of Easton. Let's face it, evangelism is simply what it says: "Go tell others," and do so by showing them how blessed you are through the gift of hearing, knowing, sharing, and living your call to discipleship—i.e., to go and make disciples.

We frequently allude to its core principles every time we reaffirm our baptismal covenant. "Will you proclaim by word and example the Good News of God in Christ?" We cannot be the prophetic Church when we pay mere lip service or, worse yet, shy away from its fundamental place in the church's Great Commission. Often we are guilty of deferring it to other entities whose distortion and misrepresentation of its true essence has violated its fundamental

---

[87] BCP, 305.

sacredness and done violence to the virtue of our core vocation as disciples of Christ to "go into all the world."

By evangelism, what does the Church mean? The definition that I prefer, which comes from the writings of Paul and the Gospel of John, is this: "making others ambassadors and friends of Christ" (2 Corinthians 5:20; cf. John 15:14). Paul W. Chilcote and Laceye C. Warner have edited a book entitled *The Study of Evangelism: Exploring a Missional Practice of the Church*, a compilation of thoughts on the subject by several renowned theologians in the academy. In their analysis, Chilcote and Warner advocate, evangelism is a vital part of something larger than itself, namely, the *missio Dei* (mission of God). While evangelism is but one part of God's larger mission in the world, it is the essence—the heart—of all Christian mission. Evangelism is a process. Making a Christian is a process that takes place over a long period of time …. Evangelism is a process more than it is an event.[88]

This definition cuts through the theological jargon and clearly makes the point. As one engages in making others the friends of Christ, the presupposition is that one is already a friend of Christ. This friendship with Christ begins at baptism, when individual men, women, and children become members of Christ, children of God, and inheritors of the kingdom of heaven. Through baptism, individuals take their rightful place in the family of God. This underscores the point that evangelism is not merely a personal activity, but it is equally a corporate activity, where we accept the place that God has for each of us in his body in the world, the church.

At the center of the Church's life is obedience to Christ, who is Lord of the Church. Evangelism is the Church's obedient response to Christ, who commands the apostles of every age to go

---

[88] Paul W. Chilcote and Laceye C. Warner, eds., *The Study of Evangelism: Exploring a Missional Practice of the Church* (Grand Rapids: William B. Eerdmans, 2008), xxvi.

into the world and make of all peoples his disciples by preaching to them the good news (Matthew 28:19). As the Church continues to live out this mandate, it must remain faithful to the Great Commission from Jesus.

We witness in the Acts of the Apostles the early church paradigm, a community of believers who formed themselves into the Church. What was special about this group of believers was their concern for each other's spiritual and material development: "They devoted themselves to the apostles' teaching and fellowship, to the breaking of bread and the prayers" (Acts 2:42). They also sold their goods "and distributed the proceeds to all, as any had needs" (vs. 45). This does not mean that the spiritual part of any person was devalued or reduced in any way. On the contrary, it meant that the individual, as both body and soul, was important.

Evangelism was important to the church then because through its evangelistic thrust, the church demonstrated that it cared for the totality of the person. This spirit characterized their concern for the spiritual and material development of their fellow human beings. These early Christians understood that the individual, as both body and soul, was important for the larger community. They understood very early in the discipline of evangelism that this pioneering community of faith needed to address the whole person as an irreplaceable component in the ministry of evangelization if it was serious in its effort to make any consequential impact in conversions.

The question of evangelism should occupy a front and center position in the Church's message. This is my snapshot of a church that is undergirded by evangelism. Importantly, it is significant to recognize that every church is located in a particular mission field; every church is called to witness for Christ in its particular context. This factor often defines the constituency or people to whom the church is called to minister Jesus's love and hospitality.

This determination will inform the shape of any church's witness. However, here are some general strategies from my experience, which I have used and found helpful in bringing people into the church but also, more importantly, in transforming them into disciples. It is decisively important for the church to have a well-defined identity and vision that parishioners find comfortable, because ultimately, they are the channels through which its message intersects the community.

Worship and music in many churches are viewed as two of the main reasons people attend church. Worship and music demonstrate in a public way the uniquely solemn, attractive, and meaningful liturgical and sacramental order of our worship service. It freezes us, so to speak, in a state of wonder, praise, and glory and transfixes us in communion with God, who, though beyond us, still lives among and through us. This must be complemented with a profoundly inspiring sermon. Worshippers must leave church uplifted and inspired.

Spare no effort and time in educating lay people to empower them as ministers. This strategy gives them not only a share in the evangelistic thrust of the parish but also ownership in the parish's direction. Opportunities for ministry are an imperative that must not be overlooked. Provisions should be made to care for young families through childcare, Christian education for all ages, youth events, acolytes' ministry, and others as may be appropriate.

Effective observance of the various liturgical seasons, allowing people to experience the rich variety of expressions available to the church, will also help. It serves to make liturgy more attractive and can go a long way to counter comments about the monotony of our worship. This strategy may be termed "in-reach evangelism" whereby discipling of the faithful is aggressively promoted.

It is important to make church a place of welcome; this inviting atmosphere must begin with curb appeal, welcome signs, and a user-friendly website with all the relevant information for anyone seeking a church, even to the warmth coming from members. Visitors should be provided with guidance in navigating our worship books. A well-trained usher ministry can make a difference in how friendly and welcoming your church is perceived to be.

Strive to be a prayer-centered, mission-shaped church invested in all possibilities that can diminish suffering through many partnership and outreach activities. It is my experience that when a church loses its vocation or purpose and focus in God's mission, it loses its soul and missional center and begins to disintegrate from within. Generally, the first to get crushed are the clergy and leadership.

Equally important is the teaching of Christian stewardship as a lifestyle discipline, rather than an activity for the solicitation of funds. Conversion of the heart translates to conversion of the "pocket." Jesus taught that "where your treasure is, there your heart will be also" (Matthew 6:21). The church should be vigilant in highlighting all major events in the life of the congregation. The Church must also be seen as rooted and grounded in prayer and spiritually focused. Clergy and vestry must give leadership in making church the place where people want to be. Challenge your church to revision and promote itself as the neighborhood church by opening its facility for creative community wide activities.

Finally, work diligently to make church a safe space for all, and boldly advertise and promote it as such. Of equal importance, deal expeditiously with potential conflicts before they get out of control. I can assure you, people love being part of a successfully faithful Church, and you will clearly notice the energy and excitement around that feeling.

The Christian community should strive to be seen and known as a church that lives and breathes reconciliation because as Christians our motivation and discipleship distinguish us as "reconciled reconcilers." There is another reason why evangelism is of great importance to the Church: though our discipleship involvement in evangelism, we are constantly renewed, strengthened, and better equipped for more effective service, sharpening the skill to point others to Christ by constantly exploring diverse ways to effect it.

In the spirit of the Inter-Anglican Standing Commission on Mission and Evangelism, one of the commissions of the Anglican

Communion, I am reminded that fruitfulness of mission is determined not necessarily by measured results but by faithfulness to Christ, believing that in Jesus God has won the victory and will overcome the world.

At the risk of repeating myself, in this connection it's time for us as a Church to be courageous and bold about evangelism. Let's reclaim it, let's reaffirm it, and let's redeem it from all its unfortunate, irresponsible publicity and gross misrepresentation and commit to return it to its prominent place within the fabric of the missional messianic church and our Episcopal Church ethos. We should be excited to embrace the truth about our call from Jesus to be evangelists.

The spirituality of the clergy, insofar as this theme is concerned, is the unequivocal acknowledgment that this is a discipline in shared ministry, the affirmation of collaborative ministry with laity. New Testament theologian William Countryman, Episcopal priest and professor of New Testament, views the place of the laity as deriving from incorporation in Christ through the water of initiation. In his opinion the priesthood of Christian people needs to be interpreted and understood in terms of Jesus's experience. Christians receive their role and place in the body of Christ, and with it comes the manifestation of gifts, which are to be used in contributing to the life of society. Countryman regards the Christian's priesthood as establishing the faith community on the borders of human existence. In fact, priesthood operates at the level of every human being, based on the premise that everyone has gifts and that everyone is introduced to *arcana*—'hidden things, secrets.'[89]

To fully understand the crucial role of the spirituality of baptism, in which all baptized are incorporated into the identity of Christ and their union within that relationship (Ephesians 2:11–22), may well be challenging for clergy spiritual formation

---

[89] L. William Countryman, *Living on the Border of the Holy: Renewing the Priesthood of All* (Harrisburg: Morehouse Publishing, 1999), 3.

in many Anglican Communion dioceses. This is particularly true in the Diocese of Seychelles and even more distinctly so in the dioceses of the Province of the Indian Ocean (Seychelles, Madagascar, and Mauritius) and some dioceses in the Province of the West Indies that are fundamentally clergy-centered in pastoral and parochial configuration. In general, the spirituality of clergy in some instances may require some deconstruction in order to accommodate intentional evangelism and robust discipleship.

Additionally, there should be a process of reorientation of the prevailing mind-set of laity, which projects the impression that ministry is the job of the clergy alone. The authority given to the evangelists is given by God. And it is God who works in and through the Church. The hierarchical ecclesiological attitude in evangelism, where "I do my own thing and on my terms," obstructs the will and work of God in our communal lives. This attitude, unless it is abandoned, poses the greatest hindrance to the Church's endeavors to evangelize the world for Christ.

The growth of the Church will be reflected in the emergence of an enlightened laity, which if aggressively and skillfully pursued may present a remarkable opportunity for the growth of the church. Consequently, this development will leave clergy free to attend to their primary function, which is to be those who administer and animate the sacraments of the Church, including the proclamation of God's sacred words. Robert Brungs develops this thought by pointing out that the Church through her ministry of sanctification, through liturgy, must foster the Christ-life of her members .... Sanctification, union with Christ, is the bond that holds the people of God together .... [The member] will find that this Christ-life in him will live only when he shares it with others, in love, in communal worship, and in all the multitude of activities in which he engages himself.[90]

---

[90] Robert A. Brungs, *A Priestly People* (New York: Sheed and Wand, 1968), 70–71.

The activity of the Church is the activity of Jesus's redeeming work, led and sustained by the power of the Holy Spirit. There is a level of spiritual empowerment in the life of the clergy when lay people are offered opportunities not merely to own their ministries but to carry them out with authority and integrity. The desire of the laity to be involved at almost every level of our diocesan life is probably one of the most positive signs of growth in global Anglicanism.

Allowed to continue, the mission of God in the church will reflect more and more what clergy potentially are called to be, that is, the community of the reconciled in a hurting nation, a nation that still looks to the clergy for leadership in Christian witness. Christ calls every baptized person to be transformed into a "reconciled reconciler." Clergy and lay are able to communicate this altruism through social advocacy and engagement in the overall well-being of the neighborhood.

Social Outreach and Advocacy

They would sell their possessions and goods and
distribute the proceeds to all, as any had need.

—Acts 2:45

"Will you seek and serve Christ in all persons,
loving your neighbor as yourself?"[91]

"Will you strive for justice and peace among all
people, and respect the dignity of every human
being?"[92]

---

[91] BCP, 305.
[92] Ibid.

By vocation Christians are agents of social change. This occupation with the community is integral to their vocational commitment to maintain *koinonia* (holy fellowship) and *balance*. In the language of spiritual formation, evil is the disembodiment of self from other, that is, community. Henri Nouwen observes, "It almost seems that being both an agent for social change and a Christian becomes a contradiction."[93] He issues this comment fully conscious of the temptation to be conceited and self-righteous in a world that offers a minefield of injustice and societal ills. However, it is his firm conviction that the way to deal with this dilemma is to begin with self. In his wisdom he offers this advice, "that for them the only real place to start changing the world is to start in the center of their own lives."[94] It is not unusual to confront people regularly who continue to feel that their actions, good or bad, have little or no consequence to the wider world. However, monasticism attaches a global view to every action regardless of its scope or magnitude. In effect, all our actions have universal ramifications.[95]

One of the fundamental responsibilities of the church is to provide for the spiritual welfare of every human being. However, the Church must strengthen its vocation to be involved in social outreach and advocacy if it is to demonstrate the sincerity of its care for the poor and needy, the marginalized and those unjustly treated. The spiritually sensitive Christian will consciously or unconsciously be drawn into action as a direct result of this spiritual dimension. This experience invariably gives rise to moral imperative in that, once clergy and lay have a sound spiritual background, they will realize the necessity for proper character formation based on the principles of honesty, humility, love, decency, respect for others, and the inalienable rights of each

---

[93] Henri Nouwen, *Creative Ministry* (New York: Image Books Doubleday, 1971), 82.

[94] Ibid., 83.

[95] Joan Chittister, OSB, *Wisdom Distilled from the Daily: Living the Rule of St. Benedict Today* (San Francisco: HarperCollins, 1991), 70.

person. When these principles are upheld, the base of spiritual formation is strengthened, which then penetrates into the wider community.

The Church's social advocacy arises out of the clergy's own heightened spiritual formation and obedience to Christ, the archetype of social outreach and advocacy. The response may not necessarily be overwhelming. One area explored for the Church in Seychelles, which received much attention, was a counseling center to assist members and others who were affected and troubled by many social problems affecting family and nation. As a result, citizens of Seychelles who often turn to the Church in times of crisis and who often hold the Church in high esteem had a true model of Christ to follow. The Church is always mindful that one of the spiritual responses in covenantal living is the education of people. In this thrust, it may be both spiritually prudent and practically sound to challenge people to accept their responsibility to make positive contributions to society. In this area, the Church's role in Seychelles as the authoritative facilitator was accessed to influence and shape the process.

A frequent proposition is for the Church to deal more with issues that are affecting society, depending on the nature of the problem. The response of the early church to the crisis at hand was to care for the needy members in the community. In the modern scheme of societal concerns, social outreach and advocacy may be best advocated through strong emphasis on the family and family-related issues. In this way, the church will play a critical part in the development and nurturing of family. The Church could do this by instilling within family members a deep-seated respect for their God-given worth and dignity which, in turn, would enhance their relationship with friends and other groups of people (e.g., coworkers). From this position of strength will flow the desire from parishioners to develop mechanisms of restraint in the face of everyday temptations. People need constant affirmation of the high premium God places on them as God's creation and people.

The spirituality of the Church takes into account the need to support and even help eliminate, where necessary, the material needs of the less fortunate. It should set aside funds to assist needy families and have an ancillary unit to support and respond to those needs. In that way, families undergoing economic hardships or otherwise unable to provide for themselves would have the support of the church and the wider community. Through this medium, fundamental social and economic reforms may be addressed in the creation of a stable family life and safe home environment.

All these possible solutions require a strong, positive, sensitive, and caring attitude from both clergy and parishioners. Once these conditions are set in place, the church should begin teaching people, to provide them with valuable information that will guide and prepare them to courageously face the challenges of the outside world.

Spiritual development is important. However, the Church must also remember to rise above this to challenge and strengthen all facets of the whole human person. Each component must be developed to the same degree if human beings are to have a balanced life and the Church family is to grow into a powerful unit in society. The Church will thus find itself in a better position to make invaluable contributions to society and all its attendant structures.

The fundamental message of the gospel is "good news to the poor" and "release to the captives" (Luke 4:18–19). In the wisdom of Benedict this activity should be cultivated in an atmosphere that ultimately realizes transformation, a theme that is overwhelmingly stressed in Benedictine spirituality.[96] In Nouwen's opinion this challenge is best engaged through careful balance. Hence, for the Christian activist committed to social change and reform, an essential prerequisite is to attend to and care for one's prayer life.[97]

---

[96] Ibid., 72.
[97] Nouwen, *Creative Ministry*, 84.

Our radical call is to embrace society with an adequate vision of what constitutes the foundation for human dignity and fulfillment. If we are "the salt of the earth" and "the light of the world" (Matthew 5:13–14), we cannot stop short of ministering to the whole person, believing that with God everything is possible (Luke 1:37) while waiting for the kingdom of God to erupt in plentitude. The spirituality of the Christian community, the Church, and clergy commits them to announce this kingdom by preaching the gospel, healing the sick, and reproving the evil spirits manifested in the reality of injustice, inequality, oppression, marginalization in all forms, and indignity. In its pursuit to fulfill the principle of human rights, the church has consistently advanced the dignity of all human beings through various tangible and transformative projects. The is the least we can do as the body of Christ in fulfillment of our baptismal covenant.

CHAPTER SIX

Ancient Spiritual Disciplines for Leadership Formation

A Rule of Life

Awe came upon everyone, because many wonders
and signs were being done by the apostles.

—Acts 2:43

"Give them an inquiring and discerning heart,
the courage to will and to persevere, a spirit to
know and to love you, and the gift of joy and
wonder in all works."[98]

Pastoral life, whether speaking of clergy or lay leaders with care
responsibility, is worked out within the fabric of service and
servanthood. As the pastoral leader engages the day-to-day care
of the faithful in a loving, humble, approachable, sacrificial, and
visionary way, the routine or daily rhythm becomes mutually
beneficial. Leading from in front, congruent with the paradigm of
the Good Shepherd, necessitates holistic articulation embodied
and enthroned in spiritual discipline. The integrated approach to

---

[98] BCP, 308.

ministry from this perspective is an implicit reality in the life of the pastor.

Our ministry, as leaders, is toward the world and has a missiological implication: it is not done for self but for the world. If the body of Christ is alive and vibrant in the world, people will be drawn to it. The classic illustration of this was in reference to early church believers: "See how these Christians love each other." Undergirding this is the fundamental belief that all the baptized have a calling to ministry, and with that comes the gift of the Spirit. In the design of Benedictine Spiritual Discipline, the "Gift of the Spirit" gives rise to a mature attitude of "Fruit of the Spirit" (Galatians 5:22–26). The profoundly transformative impartation of the Spirit in cultivating new experiences was what emboldened the faith of the emerging early Christian church community. The early believers, written about in the book of the Acts of the Apostles, witnessed the work of the Holy Spirit in its power in the form of wind and fire, the liberator who brought freedom manifested in courage illustrated by the apostles' actions. The work of the Holy Spirit gave those early believers through prayer the power to heal, the ability to release prisoners from captivity, and the gift of ethically transforming the world through the virtues of love, joy, and peace. Here manifested is the test of authentic spirituality which transforms life; this ineffable character transcends speech and imparts love.[99] This vibrant interaction of Spirit and belief cultivates the field for ministry that is faithful to world leaders who are called to serve.

In sixth-century morally bankrupt Rome, Saint Benedict offered a model in what is commonly referred to as the *Benedictine Rule of Life*. His *Rule of Life* places emphasis on a twelve-step formula for daily living, aimed at formation of the spiritual life of the monks in his monastic community. However, significant work has been done over the years by many scholars to refine

---

[99] Kenneth Leech, *True Prayer: An Introduction to Christian Spirituality* (London: Sheldon Press, 1980), 62–63.

and redesign it to suit varying contexts in the modern world, including other monastic orders, parochial liturgical formation, and lay participation, so that this foundational work even benefits people with hectic lifestyles.

As a practitioner, I could quite easily catalogue a series of fruitful results, insofar as personal spiritual engagement and transformation are concerned. When I served as parish priest in North Abaco, Bahamas, a multipoint parish configuration of six congregations with a total membership of over six hundred baptized members over a hundred-mile driving radius, I was also starting a new congregation and building a new church edifice, including raising over five hundred thousand dollars to cover the cost of construction because the new church membership wouldn't qualify for a mortgage (in fact, the parish priest and parishioners solemnly pledged to avoid pursuing a mortgage). Additionally, I was teaching twenty-one one-hour sessions to eight classes totaling 120 high school students every week and attending courses in an adult learning format during the January and June semester for three consecutive years at Colgate Rochester/Bexley Hall Seminary, Rochester, New York, studying for a Doctor of Ministry degree. This arrangement also included being a responsible and present father to our two children and a supportive and loving husband to my beloved wife.

If I may say so myself, all these responsibilities were fruitfully carried out without neglecting my duty to any of them. The discipline of a grounded spiritual practice informed by an interior life of spiritual engagement with God fruitfully guided me through this period. This is one illustration of several from a life lived in the spirit of multitasking.

From my personal conviction and practice, you could imagine my overwhelming passion and endorsement in commending *A Rule of Life* and sharing it with the clergy and laity in the diocese as a resource to add into ongoing spiritual formation. The fascinating character behind the Rule is the ripple effect it can have on all of one's life. It focuses attention on movement away from activism, which immerses us in every activity, instead helping us see life and daily activity as an intricate weaving of the spiritual, physical, and social threads of the human enterprise.

The life of any spiritually driven individual cannot escape the fundamental importance of *prayer*. This phenomenon is a common characteristic in the formal public witness of liturgy and in private and common devotion. The essential wisdom in prayer serves to shape any form of contemplative discipline and is the sum of our relationship with God. We are what we pray. The degree of any fruitful faith is measured by the degree of prayer. Prayer is listening to and responding to God by thought, word, and deed, with or without words. The very spirit is our source and reality of prayer, particularly in an unceasing rhythm. God is already at prayer in us, "for we do not know how to pray as we ought, but that very Spirit intercedes with sighs too deep for words" (Romans 8:26). Benedictine spiritual discipline promotes prayer as an avenue to help the practitioner grow into awareness of and sensitivity to God's Spirit praying in us.

Critical elements to the *Rule of Life* are *work* (asceticism) and *leisure*. It introduces a process that trains the body for self-denial or austerity. Asceticism is for the health and vitality of the body of Christ. Leisure refers to rest or the biblical use of the term *Sabbath*. Of equal importance is the time spent in *solitude*—the time spent in silence and stillness—and *community*. Solitude is the alternative to loneliness, which is the fruit of brokenness and sin.

Poverty reminds us that we have no private ownership of anything. Cardinal Basil Hume uses dependence and permission to locate the element of poverty in the tradition. Inasmuch as it is a matter of simplicity, he writes, it is "most of all a sense of dependence—dependence upon God, dependence on the Community … as an act of recognition that ultimately all things come from God. This is where the role of permission comes in."[100]

---

[100] Basil Hume, OSB, *The Intentional Life: The Making of a Spiritual Vocation* (Brewster, MA: Paraclete Press, 1977), 50.

Every activity requires permission, and that acknowledgment honors the providential grace of God, the source of all things. In his view, while living in community life, one should seek permission even to use objects belonging to the community.[101]

Chastity orders our thinking and action in the way of priority and engages intentional and focused attention on that which is useful. The exercise of *obedience* is used within the context of listening and hearing for discernment. Associated with obedience is the call to trust in the authority of the voice. *Stability* invites us to accept our position and location and tolerate the condition under which we labor. In a word, offer faithful and dedicated service wherever you are planted. *Humility* involves both heart and appearance. *Hospitality* is the extension of mutual love. Respect of the neighbor and proactive approach to the stranger and needy are fundamental prerequisites of this exercise. I wish to clearly note that the quality of hospitality is paramount in any spiritually driven person.

Spiritual Discipline of Prayer

As I continue to discern my own ministry, I have come to the realization of how special the daily Eucharist is to my spiritual formation. In parish ministry and now in episcopal ministry, it is not uncommon to attend daily Morning Prayer and Eucharist and end the day with either Evening Prayer or Compline. I have discovered this to be a daily necessity for my spiritual life, as well as for the people of God under my care. Cyril of Alexandria assesses the importance of the Eucharist this way: "For by it, Christ in us silences the law which rages in the members of our flesh, kindles piety toward God, and deadens our passions. Not imputing our transgressions to us, He heals us."[102] Hence, the Eucharist becomes

---

[101] Ibid.

[102] Peter E. Gillquist, *Designed for Holiness: God's Plan to Shape and Use You for His Kingdom* (Ann Arbor: Servant Books, 1986), 79.

the most ultimate union with Christ: in it we become divine, and through it we obtain interior strength for the challenges of the world.

The practice of *regular prayer* shapes the life of clergy and lay in ways that impact their very character as persons of faith in leadership. St. John Chrysostom makes careful note of this challenge to the priesthood. He warns of the importance of vigilance to sin in its diverse facets, even in the smallest detail. As John Chrysostom reminded his congregation, "that small offence casts a shadow over all the rest of his life."[103] The Office of Priesthood places him in an inordinate state of public scrutiny. In the wisdom of John Chrysostom, "Everyone wants to judge the priest, not as one clothed in flesh, not as one possessing a human nature, but as an angel exempt from the frailty of others."[104]

Furthermore, because the clergy is perceived to be a moral lighthouse, their character is naturally modeled by observers; likewise their foibles. In the words of Chrysostom, "The priest's shortcomings simply cannot be concealed."[105] Part of the spirituality of clergy constrains them to carry an impeccable countenance. In the description of Chrysostom, "[They] must be dignified yet modest, impressive yet kindly, masterful yet approachable, impartial yet courteous, humble but not servile, vehement yet gentle, in order that [they] may be able calmly to resist all these dangers."[106] The ultimate duty of clergy is the preservation of the church's integrity and edifying quality. The discipline of prayer and the regular engagement will bear fruit over the long haul—fruit that will eventually resemble this constellation. In the context of theology, Jesus confides in us, "Apart from me you can do nothing" (John 15:5; cf. Matthew 5:48; Romans 7:24f).

---

[103] St. John Chrysostom, tr. Henry Davis, "Six Books on the Priesthood" (Crestwood : St. Vladimir's Seminary Press, 1977), 86.
[104] Ibid.
[105] Ibid., 85.
[106] Ibid., 93.

In his contribution to the Benedictine Spirituality, Robert Benson notes the critical place of prayer in daily practice. "The heart of the prayer life that is proscribed by the Rule of St. Benedict is known as the *Opus Dei*—the Work of God."[107] For both clergy and lay, the Rule of St. Benedict weaves prayer into the time of work.

Spiritual Discipline of Work (Asceticism)

Benedict in his wisdom reminds us of the danger idleness poses to the unoccupied mind. "Idleness is the enemy of the soul."[108] In his estimation, meaningful work provides the antidote for idleness by offering the soul the opportunity to give full expression to co-creatorship for growth and change. Joan Chittister confirms *work* (asceticism) to be integral to the monastic discipline and natural activity to the life of monasticism. Her view is that "work is not a punishment or a penance. Work is a privilege."[109] Furthermore, there is a spirituality associated with this activity which promotes the countervailing pursuit of work. Work enables material and social progress implicitly to achieve the objective, which is "to get more human and to make my world more just."[110]

Asceticism (work) is the training of the body to exercise self-denial or austerity. In the ordering of Benedict's *Rule of Life*, pastoral leaders become overtly conscious to incorporate this element, because as disciples we are expected to reflect this in the way we live. In the pattern and example of the apostle who used the model of the athlete with emphasis on self-control, a punishment that is exercised for greater work can become an activity that pushes us to the limit but bears fruit for the body (1 Corinthians 9:24–27). Although this process of spiritual discipline may seem masochistic

---

[107] Robert Benson, *A Good Life*, 19.
[108] Chittister, *Wisdom Distilled*, 85.
[109] Ibid., 82.
[110] Ibid., 83.

to many people, it offers ascetic benefits for the greater good, that is, for the health and vitality of the body of Christ.

The apostle Paul's analogy of the body of Christ interprets the body to be a community (1 Corinthians 12:12–31; Ephesians 4:4–16). The gift of "charisms" or "giftedness" within its fellowship contributes to the holistic nurturing of each one for the work of ministry. This is the Pauline recipe for the orders or functions of ministry to do the work, and any deliberate effort at circumventing this process robs the laity and burdens the ordained. Joan Chittister reminds us, "Work is a Christian duty."[111] The activity of work is likely to bear fruit in spiritual maturation for the laity when their efforts are honored and redeemed.

The asceticism implied in 1 Timothy 4:6–10 enjoins the pastoral leader, as an ascetic, to explore sound teaching as a perquisite of the faith journey. The hard work of Christian education, writing, and reading is an ascetic activity. It should be remembered that the spiritual life is not compartmentalized, in that it is also a healthy blend of the many manifestations of life. This means making time for prayer, study, visiting, and so on. It means more than having a clear idea of the priorities of pastoral work. All this will require what amounts to a form of courage to fend off and to defer seemingly pressing matters, resisting the temptation to believe that all ministries must be instant.

When clergy work alone in a parish, they alone have to strike the necessary balance between *asceticism* (work), *leisure*, and *prayer*. In the spiritual life, clergy learn that to know self is an essential element for interior growth—to know one's strengths as well as weaknesses, to know one's God-given gifts as well as one's limitations. From this process clergy will grow to have a realistic assessment of their capacities and energies, so that they can approach the use of time with a view to pace themselves to

---

[111] Ibid., 85.

work at a rate they can sustain, allowing for the natural tendency to work in bursts of energy followed by periods of reduced activity.

Thomas Green is convinced that any pursuit of a deep and abiding spirituality should take cognizance of asceticism. In his analysis, this theme in the rhythm of life offers a training module to overcome or bring into submission areas of weakness and to build the strength of will to resist the devil.[112]

When it comes to leisure time, there is a need for a clear understanding that our recreational activities are not optional but essential—as important an element of our rule as is our time of prayer. For our recreation is a means of our re-creation and consequently has a great deal of bearing upon our spiritual health. The biblical correlation comes to us in the observance of the Sabbath. What is perhaps more important is the choice and ordering of the Sabbath, for it is to be leisure that absorbs, satisfies, and fulfills but does not consume us. It is to some extent a wholesome reflection of the past week and a commitment to effectively redeem the ensuing week(s).

The good ordering of our time with its balanced variety of prayer, work, and leisure will help us recharge both the spiritual and the physical batteries. Not enough stress is laid upon the need for physical stamina and endurance for those who enter the priesthood. There is also need to be reminded of the impact of the spiritual life in certain stages upon the physical resources of the body. Leisure in monasticism is perpetuated as an embodiment of work rather than separation from it and takes into consideration the state of mind toward prioritizing the day. Leisure allows us to have time not to be busy, and this non-busy time gives us time to listen to one another. A cursory review of the events surrounding Jesus's visit to the house of Mary and Martha, and the subsequent

---

[112] Thomas Green, SJ, *Prayer and Common Sense* (Notre Dame: Ave Maria Press, 1995), 100.

advice of Jesus to Martha, offers a benchmark for the healthy engagement of leisure (Luke 10:38–42).

In the wisdom of Benedict, it helps to fashion the reflective content of what is done for the world within the whole design of life's engagement. Benedictine spirituality sees leisure as an essential part of its spirituality.[113] Eugene Peterson views it as an activity that opens itself to the art of listening, an important ingredient of the pastoral life. "Pastor listening," says Peterson "requires unhurried leisure …. [L]eisure is a quality of spirit, not a quantity of time. Only in the ambience of leisure do persons know they are listened to with absolute seriousness, treated with dignity and importance."[114]

Spiritual Discipline of Solitude

In pursuit of vocation, the stillness or quietness illustrated in the practice of Jesus to withdraw into the desert to pray should be pursued in order for the clergy to engage self. The element of *solitude* or *quietness* in the clergy's *Rule of Life*—the time spent in silence and stillness—is essential: waiting on God in quietness, removing from the mind as much as possible discursive prayer and mental images, and being content to be before God. This allows the clergy or lay practitioner's soul to encounter God and be anointed with grace and healing at a level beyond comprehension or consciousness.

Mother Teresa was once asked about her prayer life, "When you pray, what do you say to God?" She replied, "I don't talk, I simply listen." Believing he understood what she had just said, the interviewer next asked, "Ah, then what is it that God says to you

---

[113] Joan Chittister, *Wisdom Distilled*, 97.

[114] Eugene Peterson, *The Contemplative Pastor: Returning to the Art of Spiritual Direction* (Grand Rapids: William Eerdmans Publishing, 1989), 21.

when you pray?" Mother Teresa replied, "God also doesn't talk but simply listens."

There was a long silence, with the interviewer seeming confused and unsure what to ask next. Finally, Mother Teresa broke the silence by saying, "If you can't understand the meaning of what I've just said, I'm sorry; but there's no way I can explain it any better."

Solitude needs the relationship of community, and this in the life of clergy or lay becomes the antidote for loneliness. The communal dimension speaks clearly to the importance of abiding in Jesus: "Apart from me you can do nothing" (John 15:4–5). Christianity is a dialogical religious phenomenon in worship and witness. We see this translated in the ministry of Jesus, who sent out his disciples, two by two, into the villages and communities. Our Lord provides a perfect illustration of shared leadership which is fundamental to communal engagement.

Spiritual Disciplines of Poverty, Chastity, and Obedience

The elements of *poverty*, *chastity*, and *obedience* form part of the classic vows of the religious order and are considered to be fruits of the activities of practice.

In secular settings the term *poverty* is generally understood to be the complete renunciation of materialism. The monastic community has worked to redeem the discipline to mean the renunciation of private ownership, in the recognition that everything belongs to God. Poverty in the language of faith and practice of life in the Spirit is connected to the theme of spiritual detachment and plays heavily on that practice. In calling the rich young ruler to sell his property, give the money to the poor, and then come and follow him, Jesus gave a fundamental message to all—to detach ourselves from the inordinate preoccupation with material and other things that have a claim on us in idolatrous ways (Luke 18:18–30).

This sense of detachment is part and parcel of the fact that we cannot take anything with us. It is an attitude that will nourish our being for the poor. The undergirding principle associated with this theme is to teach that we should not have a sense of entitlement but rather share. The Christian spiritual discipline of poverty is rooted in the discernment of how much is enough and sets in motion the unburdening of self by giving away what we have. More attention needs to be given here, especially when considering what constitutes Christian stewardship, while living in a land of inordinate abundance. This attitude is more likely than not to bring rhythm and balance in community.[115]

The spiritual theme of *chastity* could be related to a decent, modest lifestyle. It could also refer to cleansing or purgation, which has baptismal overtures. The English word *chaste* comes from the Latin *castus*, meaning "pure." In our pervasively sexual society, this theme would ordinarily be associated with abstention from sexual intercourse. However, monasticism takes it beyond this limited understanding. Chastity becomes rooted in terms of contemplation, which means to pay attention to one thing that is useful. Martha's failure (Luke 10:38-42) was not a moral failure but rather a distraction from that which was better. In a broader sense, it calls us to purge ourselves from all the distractions that keep us from God in Christ.

The spiritual theme of *obedience* in Benedictine spirituality complements humility, a natural progression in the profession of Christ above all.[116] In the community obedience is generally associated with deference to the one in authority, the abbot or bishop.[117] However, in a world that bears the scars of extensive abuse and misuse of power in every sphere of life, it may be useful

---

[115] This is a distillation of material from Professor Jonathan Linman's course on Spirituality and Practice of Ministry, June 2004.

[116] Timothy Fry, OSB, ed., "The Rule of St. Benedict" (Collegeville: The Liturgical Press, 1982), 29.

[117] Ibid., 30.

to begin redeeming the word. In spiritual practice the theme of obedience in interpretation and practice is integral to the discipline of hearing or listening. In this context, the restraint of speech is strongly advocated and is considered the antidote to evil speech that may lead to sin.[118] On the other hand, although obedience to superiors may be steadfast, yet it is not unilateral because one can hear from the "youngest."[119] In the spirit of debate, Benedictine spirituality allows for the voices of all to be heard, insisting that a fundamental part of obedience is asking questions for clarification. This may mean calling into question the authority of those whom you are called to hear from. This is extremely vulnerable but renewing and compassionate for the community. Inherent in this provision is an element of risk connected to hearing, which in turn evokes response. In our authoritarian society this openness is often implicitly or explicitly discouraged, depending on which sphere of society's organization you function in.

Henri Nouwen challenges Christian leaders to a new articulation or appreciation in allowing the fruit of compassion to permeate the core of authority. The essence of compassion is it breaks the bondage of implicit negative impulses we may feel for the neighbor: "The authority of compassion is the possibility of man to forgive his brother, because forgiveness is only real for him who has discovered the weakness of his friends and the sins of his enemy in his own heart and is willing to call every human being his brother."[120] In Christianity the fullness of our obedience is located in Christ. We are called to follow through hearing, assimilating, and becoming the Word.

Mission bears the notion of woundedness. As symbols of authority, the clergy aren't expected to abrogate the core virtue of compassion. In parish life they listen in silence to all sorts of

---

[118] Ibid., 31.

[119] Ibid., 93–94.

[120] Henri Nouwen, *The Wounded Healer* (New York: Image Books Doubleday, 1979), 41.

voices to sift out the gifts of the Spirit and the needs of the world. By enacting this discipline, they are able to discern and apply gifts for mission and ministry. This level of spiritual interaction raises accountability in their pursuit to support the community, at the same time giving respect to the spiritual journey of the local faith community including all people beyond that community.

Spiritual Discipline of Stability

The theme of *stability* goes beyond any feeling of restfulness or emotional calm to imply a state of steadiness and commitment to the firmness of purpose. The common elaboration in Benedictine spirituality includes practicing the spiritual gift of tolerance and characteristics of reliability and durability. In essence, Benedictine spirituality connects with the pastoral theme of fruitfulness in the vineyard in which one is planted, living in the sacrament of the presence even when a sense of wishful thinking may create moments of longing for where one could be headed.

The vows of stability harness the wondering heart of the believer, focusing it on God and revealing the face of God in every situation.[121] It is the ability to hear now despite the frustration and intolerance associated with the present realities in ministry. Stability creates space interiorly for clergy and lay to claim the present, if for no other reason than their personal spiritual health and well-being. By this attitude of tolerance and perseverance, that which once seemed mentally disengaging eventually grows. The constant encounter with the cross, Chittister reminds us, is the fulcrum of stability embodying the proof of human possibility: "The cross says we can rise if we can endure."[122]

Benedictine stability does not advocate surrendering or wavering before the challenges of life, rather meeting them

---

[121] Joan Chittister, *Wisdom Distilled*, 151.
[122] Ibid., 148.

head on, and this according to spiritual discipline is, "engaged through three central approaches: centeredness, commitment, and relationships."[123] In these three approaches, the clergy in ministry are presented with numerous unforeseen possibilities, which in some cases may tend threaten their wellness. This level of constancy associated with the theme of stability "requires us to be constant of heart and unremitting in our spiritual efforts."[124] The pledge or commitment to stability has biblical warrant in the relationship of Naomi and her daughter-in-law Ruth (Ruth 1:6). The relationship between the women reveals commitment and faith, a classic testament to the depth of relationship between two people who went through an inordinate level of pain.

In the language of Christianity, baptism becomes the first sacramental enactment in themes of commitment and faith, even if it is done in childhood. It speaks of a commitment to be part of a community which is rooted in God's stability with us: "I will not leave you or forsake you" (paraphrasing Joshua 1:5 and Hebrews 13:5).

Although the aforementioned vows are not included in ordination vows, the clergy embrace a sense of vocation to which they feel a call. Unlike a contract with time lines and stipulations, typically this is a covenantal relationship with God and God's people. Vows of stability are invoked, insofar as they involve prayer and discipline, reading and study, and seeing self in the larger context of God.

Spiritual Discipline of Humility

The definition of *humility* is noted in Paul's characterization of Jesus' self-emptying—*kenosis*. "In the form of God" (Philippians 2:6) reflects a nature of Christ that is preexistent and divine. Incarnation is for all intents and purposes the extreme limit of

---

[123] Ibid., 150.
[124] Ibid., 152.

self-denial or self-emptying. Christ's self-emptying is an exhortation to humility, and Paul's audience, the Philippian Christians, are to show humility toward people, particularly fellow followers. This expectation has extended beyond a select group to include everyone in general. Jesus's life and above all his death, in terms of obedience and humiliation, may be characterized as that of a slave. Crucifixion was a cruel form of punishment reserved for certain categories of people: slaves, robbers, rebels against the empire, and others of little or no status.

It is noteworthy that Jesus's own spirituality reveals he had it all before becoming human; he was equal with God. Nonetheless, it was a status he was conscious to preserve and never in the least exploited for his own purpose. He was careful not to take advantage of his own supreme authority for selfish ends. Instead he "emptied himself," giving himself to others in life and in death. Jesus's spirituality of humble obedience was exalted above all others. He is a model of our spiritual formation, for status is gained not through imposing our personality on others but rather by humbly sacrificing ourselves for others.

God initiates transformation by stimulating our desire to follow Jesus, inspiring acts expressing that desire, providing strength to persevere, and so on. We, in turn, respond by deciding to follow, acting on God's inspiration, and choosing to persevere. The call to "follow me" by Jesus disrupts our former allegiances and way of life. He gives us a new vocation, "to fish for people," as we share in his mission to proclaim the good news to all people.

The discipline of humility in spiritual life offers support to stability in that it reinforces the spiritual process and the awareness that one's charisms or giftedness is not superior to that of those one serves. The lack of humility is fraught with the adverse potential to insult people's sense of meaningfulness. The incarnation is the most profound embodiment of humility, which, when applied to New Testament teaching, offers positive and formative usefulness. Although the vow of humility in its more formal practice is rooted in monasticism, its fruitful practice among devout laity and clergy is a timeless practice.

The Rule of Benedict emphasizes humility in the acknowledgment of God's presence, which demands total response, avoiding pride laden with exploitative overtones, furthering the ongoing process of conversion toward spiritual growth, and recognizing the difference between humility and humiliation. Benedict sees the first as superior, in that it frees the spirit to recognize the importance of a person's place in the community and world and warns of the destructive force of self-love.[125]

In Benedict's estimation, humility is the process of a lifetime; he calls it "a ladder of humility."[126] In the journey toward humility, it is important for persons to honor who they are in the complexity of creation and redeem the inferior parts. In the final analysis, humility may be conceived as a formed behavior emerging from a disciplined life that flows from internal motivation by love and fear of God.

The natural inclination from this inner movement of the Spirit in the discipline of humility is to create an atmosphere of hospitality, particularly in response to Jesus's challenge in Matthew's Gospel concerning the treatment of the needy (Matthew 25:31–45). The writer to the Hebrews makes similar reference: "Do not neglect to show hospitality to strangers, for by doing that some have entertained angels without knowing it" (Hebrews 13:2). The Benedictine *Rule of Life* honors this as part of the disciplined prayer life (Rule 53:1; 3–4; 15). Hospitality becomes a proactive way of doing kindness to the least brother or sister. This theme has linkages to true discipleship. The apostle Paul admonishes the early church, "Contribute to the needs of the saints; extend hospitality to strangers" (Romans 12:13). In this rule the guest stands as the human face of Christ, and as Chittister

---

[125] Ibid., 54–55.
[126] Ibid., 56.

explains, Benedictine spirituality makes special provision for the stranger, the faith becoming earthed in reality.[127]

Nouwen sees the practice as creating a feeling of liberation in the life of the host.[128] In this relationship, we are challenged to step out of our world into the world of the stranger with all its attendant risks. The community of faith could be seen as the ideal environment, where relationships are likely to develop among a wide cross-section of people. Nouwen points out to us the irrefutable position of the church in bridging the gap in human relations. In his contribution he says, "The church is perhaps one of the few places left where we can meet people who are different than we are, but with whom we can form a larger family."[129] At a time when one of the familiar phrases and pursuits of the church is "seeker-friendly community," sensitivity to the reality of hospitality should feature prominently as one of the tools in evangelism.

One of the practical opportunities that could be established as an evangelism strategy in the practice of ministry is for clergy to encourage their congregations to welcome the task of walking guests through the liturgy, to orient them with the service. As the church explores it, it will do well to consider exploring more intentionally the many modes of hospitality, particularly in relation to evangelism.

In conclusion, an effective Rule of Life is a living phenomenon that permits the soul to respond to the movements of the Spirit. A good Rule of Life could benefit immensely from the counsel and support of an objective spiritual director. Such an individual role will be twofold, to provide the directee with the opportunity for regular review by an independent and impartial observer who will offer helpful critiques and periodic affirmations to the person so that they remain faithful and diligent in their spiritual journey.

---

[127] Ibid., 125.

[128] Henri Nouwen, *Reaching Out: The Three Movements of the Spiritual Life* (New York: Image Books, Doubleday, 1975), 79.

[129] Ibid., 83.

CHAPTER SEVEN

Spiritual Formation through Sharing

Reflective Sharing: *Lectio Divina*

Day by day, as they spent much time together in the
temple, they broke bread at home and ate their food
with glad and generous hearts, praising God and having
the goodwill of all the people. —Acts 2:46–47

"Give them an inquiring and discerning heart, the
courage to will and to persevere, a spirit to know
and to love you, and the gift of joy and wonder in
all your works."[130]

Christian vocation is a private commitment to God publicly
affirmed by vows undertaken in the presence of the people of
God, empowered by formal and informal training, motivated by
formation, enriched by sacraments, and lived out fully in the public
domain of the Church within the divine mandate of mission and
ministry. Interpersonal interaction with the congregants and wider
community marks an inescapable reality of Christian life which
the laity look to for leadership and guidance. How the clergy order

---

[130] BCP, 308.

their spiritual lives, and how that ordering is communicated to the laity for their digestion and practice, become the inextinguishable marks of the clergy, whose desire is to move their congregants forward in spiritually transformed lives.

Effective leadership draws inspiration from Jesus's teaching, "A disciple is not above the teacher, but everyone who is fully qualified will be like the teacher" (Luke 6:40). The spiritual maturation of clergy uncovers further depths of spiritual expression when that movement is shared with others. Collaborative learning is mutually beneficial to the clergy and the congregations.

The strategy I introduced to the clergy in the Diocese of Seychelles, which in my estimation is the least academically threatening and the most user-friendly to cultivate and practice, is the fruitful employment of *lectio divina*. This spiritual strategy is firmly grounded in the monastic tradition and practice that is widely used in nonmonastic community. It forms the basis of contemplative prayer. The principles employed are used in the preparation of sermons, spiritual direction, paintings, listening to music, and other forms of spiritual engagement. Michael Casey speaks of it as "a technique of prayer and a guide to living ... a means of descending to the heart and of finding God."[131] Richard Foster sees it as "a way of discovering our ability to be attentive to the heart of God in the Word of God."[132] It involves going into the mind at a deeper level of consciousness, eventually changing the way one thinks and approaches the world.

The mystical theology incorporated in this practice of contemplative prayer is that it consists of "meditation (*meditatio* or reflection on the words of scripture), affective prayer (*oratio* or spontaneous movement of the will), and contemplation (*contemplatio* or resting in God), divided into three separate

[131] Michael Casey, *Sacred Reading: The Art of Lectio Divina* (Liguori: Liguori Triumph, 1995), 51.
[132] Richard Foster with Kathryn A. Helmers, *Life with God: A Life-Transforming New Approach to Bible Reading* (London: Hodder & Stoughton, 2008), 73.

prayers."[133] In his observation, Paul Lawson, editor of a work entitled, "Old Wine in New Skins: Centering Prayer and Systems Theory", lamented the diminishing popularity this model had in the sixteenth-century Reformation, attributing it to hostility directed to the Roman Catholic Church and the perception that meditation was exclusively for those "truly close to God"[134] rather than the wisdom contained in the practice for transformation.

However, the resurgence of the model in contemplative practice along with wisdom gained from studies at the General Theological Seminary, Center for Christian Spirituality, have inspired my personal interest in the practice, a practice that has served to elevate my spiritual discipline and informed my parochial and episcopal ministry. The fact that this model operates in a simple, unobtrusive atmosphere of prayer and reflection that honors any insight brought to the exercise makes it attractive and inviting to clergy and laity at every level willing to engage in the art of contemplative prayer.

Scripture calls to mind the grounding of *lectio divina* which finds fertility in the spirit of the writer to the Hebrews: "The word of God is living and active, sharper than any two-edged sword, piercing until it divides soul from spirit, joints from marrow; it is able to judge the thoughts and intentions of the heart" (4:12). Scripture as the word of God becomes something like a living organism. When the priest engages it, the intention is not to study or master the text but to live it. It offers the rich encounter of power and presence of God so that the "contemplative" or "pray-er" (person engaged in the process of reflection) is mastered by the text, and God's presence becomes alive in word, speech, and language.

One of the fundamental observations associated with *lectio*

---

[133] Thomas Keating, M. Basil Rennington, and Thomas Clarke, "Finding Grace at the Center," in *Old Wine in New Skins: Centering Prayer and Systems Theory*, Paul David Lawson, ed. (New York: Lantern Books, 2001), 66.
[134] Ibid., 67

divina is that it is different from Bible study. The difference lies in the way the text is read and engaged, which leads to a vibrant encounter with it. Indeed, the nature of Bible study is to master the text to accumulate knowledge of the text. On this basis Bible study could act as an entrance into *lectio divina*, but the latter moves beyond it in asking the question, "What is the word for me and us for our time?"

In the task of applying the art of reading scripture prayerfully into practice, it is important to point out that as one enters the sacred presence, one gains deep awareness of what happens in the world. *Lectio divina* demands that the reader apply mental capacity to see what is going on within the text. Meaning is an ongoing revelation that emerges in the space between reader and text. Evocation refers to the ways in which the texts "leap out" to the reader. This experience of wrestling with the text shows the cocreative image of the reader in a responsive way. Evocations could begin to form in which meaning comes alive to events of life.

In practicing the discipline of *lectio divina*, whether in parish ministry or personal reflection, one must bear in mind its distinctness from Bible studies. One of the fundamental characteristics of *lectio divina* is that the process involves a deepening encounter with the text for healing, embodiment, upliftment, and life in the world; the engaged mind sees God in Christ encountering the world in a sacramental dimension. Reading scripture becomes more than a head trip: it is holistic, integrative, and sacramental. It not only edifies the mind but has psychological ramifications.[135] This quest for rebirth and regeneration in psychospiritual transformation involves self-examination and self-critique, leading in turn to transformation.

We need to see scripture reading in a larger communal context, not as the individualistic or reductive reading of scripture. This is so because Christ has no body but that which we inhabit as people

---

[135] Ibid.

of God. In baptism we are grafted into the body, and the Eucharist becomes that body. Reading scripturally deepens our understanding of participating cocreatively with Christ in the process as living him: "*Lectio Divina* leads to a conscious endeavor to live in accordance with the gospel to live what we read."[136] This level of textual engagement needs to be carefully analyzed by the audience and kept constantly in focus both in private and public practice.

One of the potential hurdles that may have to be crossed, by ardent believers in the authenticity of scripture, is this notion of questioning scriptural authority. This seemingly hesitant approach, understandably so, would more than likely be motivated by some sense of fear. However, what must be made clear for all participants is that *lectio divina* is not about being safe with God. It opens us to the deepest fear of suffering and deepest pathology. In this sense of openness humility is needed. The didactic practice or dialogical conversation in *lectio divina* needs highlighting, because this spiritual discipline demands adopting a manner and style of reading one is unaccustomed to.

Clergy and laity need to recognize further that as they enter into this area of questioning and wrestling with the text, they begin to enter into the realm of *meditatio* (meditation). This element introduces the exercise to the process of making connection to other scriptures or stories. The reader's response becomes activated, conjuring images from the conscious or subconscious, operative in the theology of God. What is God's word to me as a result of the text? How can I incarnate insights from the text? An important component to *meditatio* is the moment when words leap off pages or we struggle with them, asking the question, "What's it doing to me?" Dialogue gives rise to meditation. Engagement through this medium often brings about insightful discernment of the text, answers, and deeper meaning. This dialogical engagement is the very core of this meditative exercise.

---

[136] Casey, *Sacred Reading*, 63.

This type of conscientious awareness and indwelling allows for a deeper constellation and experience of God, which invariably affects the reader. In the opinion of Michael Casey, "To live in the presence of God alters our behavior and also effects a qualitative change in our experience. It is a dynamic element in ongoing conversion."[137] Dynamic interaction between reader and text evokes from the reader conscious and unconscious awareness. Here is when the reader enters into the sphere of *reminiscence*. This is the conscious awareness of making a connection with the text, and it is supported by *anamnesis*, which involves the reembodiment and reenactment of what is recalled.

Likewise, as Casey reminds his readers, "Our measure of openness to God is a means by which divine revelation enters this world to save it. We become receptors of grace with the capacity of transmitting further what we ourselves receive."[138] It would be advisable for the pray-er (the one who prays) to be aware that when a democratic spirit is introduced in scripture, we are not to presuppose any knowledge of it. We bring what we can to the text; openness, flexibility, and fluidity are needed in contemplation. This is so because much meditation and prayer happen in our consciousness.

The spirit of *lectio divina* is incarnated in our life's practice and ministry through bearing fruit. *incarnatio* (incarnation) is the assimilation of God's word deeply in our life. The Word of God penetrates us deeply in the core of being. This shows not only on our lips, but in our lives both in word and action. If *lectio divina* does not bear the fruit of incarnation in the life of faith, practice, and ministry, then it is only for one's interiority or private experience. The exercise of *lectio divina* bears fruit in strongly urging clergy and laity to promote change, and be receptacles and conduits of grace in and for the world.

---

[137] Casey, *Sacred Reading*, 72.
[138] Ibid., 43.

While this is important, the intensity of the ethical and missiological dimensions places us in God's world. Furthermore, God's word can touch us in the depth of our inner being to heal and forgive. This is where transformation and conversion begin. John Ackerman draws reference to the simple approach utilized by the early church to gather converts and empower them as they lived out the Great Commission (Matthew 28:18–20): "Disciple making includes evangelism, worship, and teaching. The early Church had none of our fancy programs. It grew disciples by their life together, prayer, fellowship, and teaching."[139]

Lectio divina results in a changed life, the outcome of which has an effect in the life of the world. When clergy and pastoral leaders have deep encounter, deep peace, less anxiety, and a deep kind of gladness, people will see it and respond to it. It is a way of putting it into your mouth, eating it, digesting it, and practicing it. The priestly office lays this burden on clergy to engage dutifully the discipline of study in order to be fruitful, thereby guarding against setting a poor example, which is likely to arise from an uninformed mind. Gregory the Great forthrightly pointed to the consequences of poor pastoral leadership, "when the subjects do not follow the instruction which they hear, but imitate only the wicked examples which they see …. For no one does more harm in the Church than he, who having the title or rank of holiness, acts evilly."[140]

Contemplation upon the heavenly opens up new vistas of spiritual awareness and responsibility for the burden placed upon the clergy's call to lead. The role of clergy as intercessors is severely interrupted when, as a result of sin, they find themselves out of favor with God.[141] The prayerful study of scripture creates the atmosphere for contemplation, which offers fertile ground to bear

---

[139] John Ackerman, *Listening to God: Spiritual Formation in Congregation* (Bethesda: The Alban Institute, 2001), 41.
[140] St. Gregory the Great, tr. Graham Neville: "Pastoral Care" (Westminster: The Newman Press, 1950), 24.
[141] Ibid., 39.

fruit of incarnation in life of faith, practice, and ministry. Roger Ferlo sees this exercise as engaging our entire sensory capacity in prayer. "Reading scripture attentively is a matter not just of sight, but also of sound and touch, even of taste and smell."[142]

The inclusive structure of *lectio divina* makes it a useful model for lay and clergy to collaborate in spiritual formation. One critical observation involved in this discipline is for participants to pay close attention to the activity taking place in the unconscious. The human personality is both flesh and mental capacity, and it is impossible to resort to one at the exclusion of the other. Contemplation is mystical union that arises out of the movement from *lectio* through to *oratio*. The moment of transformation or conversion soaks in when *lectio divina* allows the text of God's word to touch our heart and not just our head; when we begin to listen and hear Jesus comforting us: "I am with you always, to the end of the age" (Matthew 28:20). Harmony with the Word of God becomes embodied in the world and in mission. Its tangible and visible manifestation is lived out in the people's stewardship of time, talent, and treasure and made available to the kingdom of God. When we live this way there is an inherent passion emanating that compels us to engage transforming society, for social justice, or for individual acts of compassion. Contemplation, insofar as it gets us deeply into the presence of God, is to let God be God and to become who God wants us to be. As Francis Nemeck and Marie Coombs reminded us, "By virtue of the universal call to holiness every person is called to contemplative prayer: loving abandonment to God in faith."[143]

The faithful should be exposed to greater levels of biblical understanding through different forms of biblical interaction. Biblical knowledge needs to identify with the way communities

---

[142] Roger Ferlo, *Sensing God: Reading the Scriptures with All Our Senses* (Cambridge: Cowley Publications, 2002), 3.

[143] Francis Nemeck and Marie Coombs, *The Spiritual Journey* (Collegeville: Liturgical Press, 1986), 114.

can respond to their faith and the application of biblical truths to everyday experiences. The apostle Paul certainly warned the Church about the need to make the gospel available: "How are they to hear without someone to proclaim him?" (Romans 10:14). In his second letter to Timothy he again stressed the importance of teaching the Word of God as a safeguard against false teachers and advocates of heresy: "The time is coming when people will not put up with sound doctrine, but having itching ears, they will accumulate for themselves teachers to suit their own desires, and will turn away from listening to the truth and wander away to myths" (2 Timothy 4:3–4).

The spiritual formation principle embodied in scripture is equally articulated as essential for equipping the baptized for ministry: "All scripture is inspired by God and is useful for teaching, for reproof, for correction, and for training in righteousness, so that everyone who belongs to God may be proficient, equipped for every good work" (2 Timothy 3:16–17). Even if the incarnation of Christ is a once-and-for-all event, we, as the body of Christ, carry it on in our bodies. We embody the Word and become Christ for the world. It would help to be mindful that a sense of deep encounter or deep mystical union does not detach us from the world but reengages us with the world.

In looking at this spiritual discipline we see its obvious association with ethics, social justice, evangelism, and mission locally and globally. The art of *lectio divina* connects us to the entire world, thereby engaging the wholeness of who we are. In our individualistic society this inclusive engagement with the world and neighbor cannot be stressed enough, especially when during the talk of spirituality so much energy has been invested in seeing religious experience as a private affair. In the Spirit's power, we have to allow it to bear fruit—to incarnate the experience.

What more visible and tangible evidence do the faithful need to fully activate this experience than the holy Eucharist, which in effect sets the agenda for the Church? The order of the Eucharist reflects the gathering as an activity preparatory for *lectio divina*. The Liturgy of the Word relates to *lectio*; scripture acts as fodder for meditation; the sermon functions as a meditation on behalf of gathered community; and meditation is not the domain of the preacher but the work of everyone. It is the responsibility of everyone to be actively involved in preaching. The Prayers of the People are related to *oratio*; here space is open for people to add their prayers. Prayer is close to a meditation which leads to *contemplatio*, mystical experience of binding together the people of God. There is no deeper level of contemplation than to receive Jesus through flesh and blood, which is the incorporation of Jesus into our inner being, literally engaging Jesus in silence. Jesus touches those places we prefer not to visit, see, or smell. It is the deepest kind of contemplation that we can possibly experience: that we now enflesh Christ in body and blood and go in peace to serve the world. This represents the irrefutable spiritual agenda for mission and ministry as defined by the incarnation.

Models for Lay and Clergy Reflection

The model utilized in the Diocese of Seychelles to engage private devotion in the contemplative practice of *lectio divina* was offered by the Center for Christian Spirituality. It was accessed while attending a course in the introduction and practice of *lectio divina*. This model was supplemented in group parochial and diocesan practices by the adoption of an African model used in Bible study. A similar model was employed at the Bible study sessions during the Lambeth Conference of Anglican/Episcopal Bishops, University of Kent, United Kingdom, in July and August 2008. The rationale for introducing it here is to locate a model for practical approach in spiritual formation by using the contemplative practice of *lectio divina*. This is meant to offer a way forward toward an entrance into the wisdom of the model for engaging scripture.

Modeling a Practice in *Lectio Divina*

Lectio
1. Dynamic interaction between reader and text
2. Evocations (re: meaning and sacred presence)

Meditatio
3. Reminiscence
4. Anamnesis

Oratio
5. Defensive strategies
6. Appraisal of metaphor and paradox
7. Compunction
8. Aspirations

Contemplatio
9. Catharsis
10. Embodied nature of contemplative union (re: kataphatic (positive articulation) of apophatic (negative) experience

The following model approaches contemplative exercise in a more user-friendly manner and was found to be easily articulated by diocesan clergy and laity.

Model from an African Context Adopted for the Diocese of Seychelles

Opening Prayer: Blessed Lord, who caused all holy Scriptures to be written for our learning; Grant us so to hear them, read, mark, learn and inwardly digest them, that we may embrace and ever hold fast the blessed hope of everlasting life, which you have given us in our Savior Jesus Christ; who lives and reigns with you and the Holy Spirit, one God, for ever and ever. *Amen.*[144]

1. One person reads the passage slowly.
2. Each person identifies the word or phrase that catches their attention.
3. Each person shares the word or phrase around group.
4. Another person reads the passage slowly.
5. Each person identifies where this passage touches their life today.
6. Each shares.
7. Passage is read a third time (another reader).
8. Each person names or writes "From what I've heard and shared, what do I believe God wants me to do or be?"
9. Each person shares their answer.
10. Each prays for the person on their right, naming what was shared in the other steps.
11. Close with the Lord's Prayer and silence.

Rediscovering the charismatic life of the church, by reshaping and reviving the discipline of communal conversation around the Word of God, provides immense potential for stimulating the engagement of the people of God in new and exciting ways. It will provide opportunity for people to talk, to tell their own stories of faith, and to see the vision of God's love for us while at the same time creating occasions that will lead us to love each other as companions on a common journey.

Conversation around a sacred agenda allows us to take a holy moment of respect and give it opportunity for affirmation and growth. We have this charisma, for the church is the embodiment of faith which promotes companionship through collaboration and collegiality for a healthy, vibrant and well-informed, prayer-centered, and mission-shaped faith community.

---

[144] BCP, 236.

CHAPTER EIGHT

Discipleship and Spiritual Growth for Ministry

From his fullness we have all received, grace upon grace.

—John 1:16

Discipleship is a way of life that spells out one's structure of allegiance, whether it is political, ideological, spiritual, ethical, intellectual, or otherwise. It essentially requires a relentless willingness to learn, to embrace, to follow, and to represent that which is most meaningful in one's life. It generates varying levels of responsiveness both from those within its range as well as those without. Accordingly, it is possible to say that discipleship has the power to ascend to, and assume, the highest levels of human life, and conduct, and dignity, and devotion; while, at the same time, it can plunge into an inexorable descent to the lowest levels of human despair, destruction, and decay. Discipleship can be just as much the engine of radicalism as it can be the energy for spiritual vitality, moral purity, or human ascendancy.

A disciple is an avid learner, a radical follower, an embodied symbol, and a committed agent or representative. It all depends on the nature of the leader and the direction of the movement. The word *disciple* appears at least 260 times in the New Testament, mainly in the Gospels and the Acts of the Apostles. It comes from the Greek *mathetes* and the Latin *discipulus*. They both refer to persons who adhere to and are committed to teachings, ethos, doctrines, philosophies of teachers, thinkers, prominent religious figures, either in the past or in the contemporary situations. The fundamental ministry of the church above all requires of its clergy and lay leaders "leadership in the true discipleship of Jesus, with all the spirituality which this discipleship of Jesus involves in the New Testament."[145]

The most prominent scenario of discipleship in the Old Testament is between Elijah and Elisha (1 Kings 19:16–2 Kings 13). There is also the mention of the idea in Isaiah 8:16 and 50:4. Ezra is also named as having disciples. There is a school of thought that the relationship between Moses and Joshua was one of master and disciple (Exodus 24:13; 33:11; Joshua 1:1). There is the mention of the "sons of the prophets" we find in 1 Samuel 10:5–10. It is also suggested that the depth and range of the Wisdom literature, particularly in Job, Proverbs, and Ecclesiastes, would not have been sustainable without a group of thinkers and discussants wrestling with some of the deep questions of the day, particularly with respect to moral and ethical issues, the divine orientation of nature, and the wisdom found in creation. Outside of the Hebrew scriptures themselves, there is abundant evidence in Jewish communities that the rabbinical schools had fairly large followings, so that the rabbis themselves were leaders of thought and sociopolitical activity. This was certainly the context in which Jesus of Nazareth emerged as a prophetic leader and was given the title of Rabboni, by at least two Gospel characters, Bartimaeus in Mark and Mary Magdalene in John.

Jesus of Nazareth raised the level of discipleship to a very high level. He was obviously very careful in choosing his followers; and this distinguished him from the scenario of John the Baptist

---

[145] Davis, *Serving with Power*, 29.

and his disciples. The main distinction was that whereas John's disciples chose to follow him of their own volition, Jesus specifically chose his own and invited them to follow him. What made life even more interesting was that the disciples who first joined the Jesus movement at the invitation of Jesus then went after other recruits. So there emerged a dedicated band of followers over time; Matthew, Nathaniel, Phillip, James, John, Martha, Mary, Andrew, and so forth.

In the Acts of the Apostles there is abundant evidence of the diverse range of discipleship in the apostolic community, especially with respect to the way in which they were led by the Holy Spirit in bearing witness to the meaning and message of the Jesus story, particularly after the Pentecost event. There is heightened evidence in Acts that they understood discipleship to be inextricably linked with the sacred obligation to exercise their missionary zeal. Those who followed Jesus were known to be members of the Way, much more so than members of the Church as such.

Discipleship for them meant a life of movement, change, and conversion. We should be mindful that conversion is not for the faint of heart, it requires effort and perseverance. The process requires much dedication, devotion, determination, desire and discipline and these qualities are embedded within the fabric and fortitude of Christians.

This fellowship within the early church gave rise to the fourfold strategy of evangelism: house groupings, literature, missionary activity, and martyrdom. Discipleship for them involved a life of nurture and compassion, mixed with Christ-centered *kerygma* or proclamation and God-directed *didache* or teaching. It encompassed their dedication of their talents, their gifts, their opportunities, and their special brand of witness with countercultural modes of fellowship and even unjust suffering. The missionary successes of St. Paul would certainly not have been possible without the band of followers and adherents to the gospel mission who accompanied him and represented him in so many different places. His farewell address to the church at Ephesus in Acts 20 has always been one of my favorite passages in the New Testament, spoken by one who was clearly not just a missionary but indeed a master-teacher in the tradition of Jesus himself, who remains for all time the Master of the master-teachers. At its highest level therefore, discipleship in the religious key is essentially an inextricable relationship between the master-teacher and the learner. The learners follow as they learn and bear witness to the transforming changes and growth marks in their lifestyle and in their ongoing experiences.

Of course, a fundamental aspect of the meaning and measures of discipleship is the obligation to become fully engaged in disciple-making. The classical mandate for this is the so-called Great Commission of Matthew 28:19–20 to go out into all the world, make disciples of all peoples, and baptize them in the name of the blessed Trinity. This has always implied that evangelism, baptism, and disciple-making are all integral parts of the same missional and ecclesial mandate. Those who are baptized are expected to live into their commitment to follow Christ, just as much as they undertake to renounce all forms and vestiges of the anti-Christ. This is to be a continuous lifestyle. The Anglican Consultative Council puts it this way: "being discipled and discipling others is a lifelong journey as we follow Jesus Christ, acting on his words, and walking in his ways towards a deeper redeemed relationship with God, being 'changed from one degree of glory to another' as we walk more closely with him and each other."[146]

Discipleship demands real sacrifice of ourselves, offering up to God that which is most precious and valuable, whether in our own eyes or in the eyes of the world. What we attempt to do for God's sake is invariably blessed by the providential grace of God to reap benefits and opportunities far beyond our wildest imagination or expectations. I believe that genuine sacrifice always leads to divine

---

[146] John Kafwanka & Mark Oxbrow, eds., *Intentional Discipleship and Disciple-Making* (London, Great Britain: The Anglican Consultative Council, 2016), 7.

success—provided that we allow God to measure that success in God's terms and not ours. Remember that God does not call us to be successful; God simply calls us to be faithful; and in doing so, we can always trust in the trustworthiness of God. So the miracle of feeding in all the four Gospels is central and pivotal to the Jesus story as well as our own. God always has the means of making our little genuine sacrifices go a very, very long way.

Discipleship demands the highest level of personal authenticity and the deepest level of genuine sincerity. Such a demand requires of us that level of trust in God, where we are always seeking to be converted to Christ, over and over again. It is the constant replay of our baptismal promise: Do you turn to Christ? The answer is: I turn to Christ every day. Sincerity demands a spiritual curiosity, a spiritual openness to God's Spirit, and the convulsive effects that will take hold of us, in season and out of season. It demands a spiritual quest to seek for Christ not only in our own encounters with each other but also in the deep searching and longings of our own hearts, minds, and wills.

The path of discipleship leads us inexorably from the point of need through the point of seeking through a fervent and regular prayer-filled lifestyle. We can reach the point of finding God afresh day after day through our resolute determination to follow Christ, even in moments and places where we would rather not go. So it demands of us a constant obedience to the will and ways of Christ; a radical sense of kenosis and self-denial for the sake of Christ; and an utter, complete, and unconditional dependence on God through Christ, who said to St. Paul, as he also says to all of us: "My grace is sufficient for you" (2 Corinthians 12:9). It raises the question then, "What more do you want?"

Finally, discipleship is a shared experience. We journey on this pilgrimage of faith together, always reminding ourselves to get rid of all excess baggage. We believe together. We are called up together both individually and collectively. We bear each other's burdens. We uphold each other in divine love, in prayer, with compassion, with generosity, in the clinics of mercy and justice, and with the joy of mutual support and inexhaustible forgiveness. It has been rightly observed that "discipleship is a call to me, but is a journey of 'we.'" Kortright Davis recognizes the individual's personal investment in their dedication to ministry: "the call to ministry as discipleship is that of personal animation, a personal restlessness in the midst of moral, spiritual, and relational crises. The disciple is driven by God's spirit to make no peace with oppression, to turn bad news into good by the power of the cross, and to demonstrate that *laborare* is truly *orare*, that is, to work is really to pray"[147]

---

[147] Davis, *Serving with Power*, 29.

CHAPTER NINE

Spiritual Transformation: A Life of Grace

Discipleship is the essence of spiritual transformation, insofar as a disciple of Christ will be likely to pursue deeper and intentional spiritual growth. Discipleship becomes productive when it engages with purpose and intentionality the struggles and nuances of the believing community. It is within the context of the community that genuine transformation becomes active witness, thereby allowing spirituality to become incarnate. John Macquarrie believes spirituality to be an activity that engages service to the community. "Spirituality is not a retreat or escape into an inner world, for spirit is precisely the capacity to go out, and the truly spiritual person is the one who is able to go out or to exist in the full dynamic sense."[148]

Ultimately, spiritual transformation, realized by the discipline of contemplative prayer, evokes for us a deeper appreciation of God who is prepared to forgive. It is helpful to understand that grace resides within our capacity to exercise our free will by giving the Holy Spirit an opportunity to be manifested in and through us. We cannot follow Jesus through our own power; we need his power, as in the Pauline confession, "I can do all things through

---

[148] John Macquarrie, *Principles of Christian Theology* (London: SCM Press, 1977), 7.

him [Christ] who strengthens me" (Philippians 4:13). Benedict Groeschel believes that the grace of God is the underlying activity undergirding spiritual life; grace, the free gift of God making us children of adoption and capable of accepting Christ as our Lord and Savior, is the vital power of spiritual life.[149]

To experience grace is to appreciate that our attitude toward spiritual formation is an essential medium that demonstrates our capacity to draw closer to Christ, who destroys sin with his love. It therefore follows that the process of spiritual formation and unification with Christ is possible only if the individual is prepared to accept the transition—with its moments of alienation, abandonment, and feelings of darkness, sin, engulfment, and dissolution—as a prelude to spiritual transformation. One should also be prepared to view this spiritual process in the same way as John of the Cross did. Michael Wasburn cites John of the Cross as interpreting it as "an indicator of authentic spiritual growth occurring."[150]

The pilgrimage to salvation and holiness takes us through this active immersion in scripture, and any identification with Jesus requires obedience even in the face of pain and rejection. In addition, this prolonged transition could represent a real experience of grace, preceded only by baptism and other related forms of initiation such as confirmation and ordination. This is recognized within the framework of transformative pilgrimage as the desire to dwell in the "holy."

As clergy and lay live out their Baptismal Covenant in everyday pastoral and liturgical practices, the depth of the interior life will act as a source of strength for their busy schedule. The likelihood for clergy "burnout" is also minimized. By living the interior life with Christ, clergy and lay educators will inevitably enrich, and

---

[149] Benedict J. Groeschel, *Spiritual Passages: The Psychology of Spiritual Development* (New York: Crossroad, 1988), 120.

[150] Michael Washburn, *Transpersonal Psychoanalytic Perspective* (Albany: State University of New York, 1994), 220.

define more astutely and intentionally, the areas of teaching given to the faithful. It is worth reiterating that clergy members, as well as lay leadership, teach and minister as persons of God who have been with God and talked with God.

With this gift for spiritual growth and empowerment comes also the capacity to adopt better habits toward other areas of life. Fiscally challenged dioceses will always face some difficulty in adequately compensating their clergy; therefore, clergy will need to exercise discipline in order to adjust to meager stipends and inadequate benefits, embracing the Benedictine mantra or principle, "Less is more." The call to inculcate an austere lifestyle, one of the classic elements in Benedictine spirituality, could serve well in benefiting clergy in the church depending on the context and country in which they may be called to give pastoral leadership.

The rhythmic balance of liturgical prayer and engagement of the daily routine, in what could be termed the sacralization of the secular, will offer opportunity for renewal and reinvigoration as leaders meet in community or in private. One of the implicit characteristics of Benedictine spirituality that should be attractive to them is that the Anglican/Episcopal Liturgy is fundamentally Benedictine in style and rhythm.

It is worth commenting that love for parish ministry is rooted in serving people. This vision represents a deliberate and linear progression, a movement of life from nothing to something. It is my conviction that within the isolated geographical location of the Diocese of Seychelles and dioceses of similar configuration in the Anglican Communion, clergy and lay leadership are encouraged to develop and practice Benedictine spirituality as it offers the discipline of the *Rule of Life*. It should be noted that the discipline of Benedictine spirituality will offer a way forward in introducing and maintaining clergy balance that is integral to fundamental spiritual formation.

When it comes to this level of quite intimate teaching, I have found that one of the necessary prerequisites has been the establishment of trust and confidence. This is achieved in two ways: first, by clergy's willingness to disclose something of themselves, of their spiritual experience and growing pains; and second, by their willingness to share in the growing process of members at an intimately spiritual level. Drawing wisdom from my personal experience has shown that the sort of spiritual exercise advanced here has greatly enhanced understanding and built fellowship.

The ministry of clergy is the direct interaction between spiritual formation and pastoral life. This understanding is assuming more and more credibility, over against a ministry that is centered and organized primarily around theological astuteness or a business model strategy. Eugene Peterson sought to reclaim this paradigm, moving ministry away from its present confinement to theological competence or business acumen, and centering it in faith and prayer. In his estimation, "Prayer is the most thoroughly *present* act we have as humans, and most energetic .... [W]e pay attention to God and lead others to pay attention to God .... It hardly matters that so many people would rather pay attention to their standards of living, or their self-image, or their zeal to make a mark in the world."[151] This is the template for ministry in which the other components such as communion, spirituality, and apostolic action are grounded.

Discipleship and the Fruit of the Spirit

Our lives as followers of Christ are like heavenly gardens on earth, where we are nurtured and enriched to bear fruit. The imagery of fruit and fruitfulness is pivotal in our biblical tradition. In Isaiah 27:6, for example, we find the prophet foretelling a pleasant future for Israel: "In days to come Jacob shall take root, Israel shall blossom and put forth shoots, and fill the whole world with fruit." In the New Testament, however, fruitfulness becomes a metaphor

---

[151] Peterson, *Contemplative Pastor*, 43–44.

for progress, growth, maturity, holiness, Christlikeness, prosperity, and fullness of the Holy Spirit. We recall Jesus's use of the Parable of the Sower (Matthew 13:18–23 and Mark 4:1–9) with the variety of yields that come from a variety of soils. We recall the story of the fig tree (Matthew 21:19) outside Jerusalem that Jesus curses to its death because of its fruitlessness.

Most particularly however, we are to be endowed with the fruit of the Spirit that is mentioned by St. Paul in Galatians 5:22ff. Those who are led by the Spirit are endowed by special qualities of character and life: love, joy, peace, longsuffering, kindness, goodness, faithfulness, gentleness, and self-control. Against all of these, he says, there can be no law. Nobody can stop you from producing such fruit. Further on in that chapter, Paul asserts that they mark out the intentional disciple as a person who is liberated from the slavery of sin. We should be mindful to appreciate that fruit is developed in a two-part process: through the believer's walk with God, and through yieldedness to the Holy Spirit. At all times, we should keep in focus that the fruit of the Spirit helps define what a Christian is.

Fruit of the Spirit is central to any notion of ministry. Scripture supplies this paradigm to measure the effective service, leadership, and character of Christians (Galatians 5:22–23). A life of faith and prayer inspired by the Spirit is the quintessential character of ministry. Ministry is synonymous with growth; it is the Spirit that activates growth within the interior life of the church. However, it may be worthwhile to stress that the fruit of ministry for the spiritual life is centered in love, the greatest of all gifts (1 Corinthians 13). Although many have argued for Christian truth, faith, religious experience, or service as the vital component of the Spirit, still, their unique place is revered in ministry. John Stott reminds us, "Love is the preeminent Christian grace."[152] In this

---

[152] John R. W. Stott, *The Contemporary Christian* (Leicester: InterVarsity Press, 1992), 146.

context the imperative is for believers to surrender themselves to the Holy Spirit in order to "live by the Spirit" and "be led by the Spirit," in order to allow the Spirit rightful sovereignty over them.

In my humble opinion, revival and renewal for the Anglican tradition resides in the spiritual life of both clergy and lay, and takes effect in formation and education given to the faithful, inclusive of continuing education clergy are willing and open to access. In light of this contribution, teaching itself is centered upon spiritual matters having to do with salvation, the knowledge of oneself and of God, and the pursuit of holiness. Our renewal and ongoing spiritual formation must involve a willingness to go back to fundamental principles embodied in the Baptismal Covenant and to teach as directly as we can the pathways of prayer, the insights of Scripture, the embodiment of Christ in the Holy Eucharist, and the necessity of God's love and grace. We need to renew our teaching materials and develop ways in which we can assist one another. It is imperative to find the time to teach more in depth and thoroughly certain groups and individuals who we hope will themselves become educators of the faithful.

This is how I would propose to approach these challenges in small dioceses facing inadequate resources, fiscal pressures, clergy shortage, and geographical constraints. The way forward is to implement simple programs that are easily accessible and inexpensive to operate. Every small diocese undergoing fiscal or resource deficits should be intentional in promoting and advocating these types of programs in spiritual formation for leadership development.

In conclusion, as we intentionally engage our call to be the Church in this generation and beyond, it will be comforting to remind ourselves that the Church has never changed its message, for the truth we proclaim is unchangeable. The Church's greatest challenge in these times is to tell the story and to correspondingly live the story relevant to this time.

The world still hungers for the authentic gospel proclaimed

from the chancel steps and pulpits of the authentic church whose qualities are inclusiveness, love, mercy, self-giving, hospitality, and the willingness to live outside of self. In this church, the spiritual core is less about self-realization and more about self-actualization; that is, in self-realization or self-awareness we feel that we have reached a place of heightened personal transformation. However, self-actualization enables us to translate that personal experience into moral, spiritual, and social lighthouses, that is, going out into the neighborhood and actually becoming broken bread and poured out wine for the world, emulating Jesus's perfect example of spiritual realization and spiritual actualization. And such a church forms people into the image and likeness of Jesus (*imago dei*), and is patience personified and grace amplified. Grace amplified is the blessing that blossoms from tending the young plant, emulating the Pauline story with his two protégés Titus and Timothy.

The Church Catholic (universal) is driven by faith and shaped by deep conviction undergirded by the humility of contrition, regular confession and daily conversion. The living church constantly realizes that the center of our unbridled spiritual optimism is a power greater than our imagination: Christ the resurrected Lord and Savior. This Church is forever mindful of this truth, that "a risen Savior is incompatible with a dying Church," in the words of Jesus, "the gates of Hades will not prevail against it" (Matthew 16:18). The Church remembers (*anamnesis*) the promise of Jesus, "I am with you always, to the end of the age" (Matthew 28:20).

Riddled by pains of despair, let the call to make disciples be this vision we pursue under the banner of Christ and the tutelage of scripture, inspired by the Holy Spirit. As I see it, the overrated refrain, "The Church is dying," should be more accurately recast as "The Church isn't dying; rather, the Church is shedding skin." It is doing so in order to take on new skin which will allow it to heal itself, rendering it more agile, vital, energized, and spirit-filled, focused on being the embodiment of Jesus, and with King David praying for "a clean heart ... and ... a new and right spirit" (Psalm 51:10).

This is a sign and signal that the Church is undergoing a healing process that in the end will result in a renewed, reinvigorated Church with a compelling vocation to be both the repository of God's love—the agent of grace and mercy, and the vessel of renewal, regeneration, and rebirth—and the dispenser of those characteristics with unfeigned loyalty and inextinguishable commitment to Jesus's way of love. Finally, it is my personal conviction informed through years of ministry in diverse missional contexts that church growth will happen when members are discipled and formed and transformed for Christ.

I find it appropriate to conclude my thoughts with a prayer that I have loved and prayed ever since I was converted to Christianity. It is a prayer attributed to the Spanish theologian Ignatius of Loyola (1491-1556) –

Anima Christi
Soul of Christ, sanctify me.
Body of Christ, save me
Blood of Christ refresh me
Water from the side of Christ, wash me
Passion of Christ, strength me
O good Jesus, hear me
Within Thy wounds hide me
Suffer me not to be separated from Thee
From the malicious enemy defend me
In the hour of my death call
And bid me come unto Thee
That I may praise Thee with Thy saints
and with Thy angels
Forever and ever
Amen!!

Returning to the New Testament Church

Acts 2:42–47

Part I: The Background of the Early Church

- **Peter's Sermon after the Pentecost (Acts 2:14–41)**
  - Peter explains the Pentecost.
    - The disciples were not drunk.
    - They were filled with the Holy Spirit.
    - This was a fulfillment of prophecy (Joel 2:28–32).
  - Peter preaches the message of the cross.
    - Jesus is exalted to the right hand of God.
    - He was crucified for us.
    - God raised him up.
  - The invitation to repent and be baptized.
    - The promise is for all.
    - Three thousand souls added to the church.

Part II: The Early Church

- **The Composition of the Church**
  - The true church as the body of Christ began on the day of Pentecost.

- It was founded upon the death, resurrection, and ascension of Jesus Christ.
- The church became one body by the baptism of the Spirit; the outpouring of the Spirit brings Christian unity.
  - The church started with 3,000 born-again believers and 120 disciples.
  - The Lord added to this number day by day those who were being saved.
  - The church was not a building.
    - It was the "called-out-ones."
    - They believed in Christ.
    - They were interwoven in each other's lives.
- **The Priorities of the New Testament Church**
  - **Teaching**
    - Spiritual babes have a tremendous need to be fed.
    - All the teaching was done by the apostles, who learned from Christ.
    - They did not have the New Testament, just the Old, and what Jesus taught them.
    - The word forms the foundation of the church.
  - **Fellowship**
    - Goes beyond refreshment after a church service.
    - It is common sharing, being a partner in projects, emotions, grief, and happiness.
    - It involves giving time, gifts, and exhortation.
    - People are involved and participating as partners in the lives of others.
  - **Communion**
    - They ate their meals from house to house.
    - They observed the Lord's death through the bread and wine.
    - They did this without the clergy and not even in a church building.

- o **Prayers**
    - Prayer was not to be a last resort when all else fails.
    - Prayer was constant and a priority in their lives (1 Thessalonians 5:17)
    - It should be the basis of everything we do.
- **Power in the New Testament Church**
    - o The church began with Pentecost (Acts 2:1–13)
        - People baptized in the Holy Spirit and speaking in other tongues.
        - When the people got together, things happened.
    - o The teaching brought a feeling of awe (v.43).
        - This was an awareness of the greatness of God.
        - Miracles took place through the apostles.
            - God worked through them so that their ministry could be authenticated.
            - Observers would know for certain that they were seeing and hearing God's men.
    - o The fellowship brought unity and unselfishness.
        - They sold their property and possessions and shared.
        - They reached out and met the needs of one another.
    - o As they ate together, they did so with gladness and sincerity of heart.
        - There was enjoyment and joy among the Christians.
        - They were not pretentious.
- **Today's Challenges for the New Testament Church**
    - o The membership is not a body of all born-again believers.
        - The makeup of our church community today.
            - **Believers:**
                - o Who accept Jesus as Savior—carnal.
                - o Who accept Jesus as Savior and Lord.

- **Nonbelievers:**
    - Who made a commitment to the church and not to Christ.
    - Who have made no commitment.
- A small percentage of the body of Christ is baptized in the Holy Spirit.
    - The church is without power.
    - Many churches deny that the Holy Spirit is for today.
- The awe and reverence of God is missing.
    - Many do not see the greatness and holiness of God.
    - Church often desecrated.
    - Communion taken unworthily.
- Not enough outreach.
    - As we give, we receive.
    - Reaching out to others is reaching out to God. (Matthew 25:35–40).
- Prayer base missing.
    - A moving church needs prayer.
    - Without prayer, we are open to the darts of the enemy.

Part III: Conclusion

What will we do about these challenges?
The church in the home is the answer:

- It seeks to bring unity in the body of Christ.
- It seeks to bring enlightenment through teaching.
- It seeks to strengthen the believers and give them communion with God through prayer.
- The power of God is evident there.

Faith - What Is It?

James 2:14–26

Introduction

Someone once said that faith is like calories: you can't see them, but you can always see their results! And that is the major theme resonating throughout James's letter: **results.** Genuine faith produces genuine works. And nowhere is this theme more passionately argued than in James 2:14–26.

Initial Clarification

There is one issue that needs clarification. That is the apparent contradiction between the thrust of our passage today (especially verse 24) and Paul's great thesis in Romans 3–5, especially 3:28; cf. Ephesians 2:8–9; 2 Timothy 1:9; Titus 3:5. We must, first of all, examine three important differences between James and Paul in their teachings on **faith.**

- **First,** the **emphasis** of Paul's and James writings is **different.** Paul stresses the root of **salvation,** which is **faith in Christ** plus nothing. James stresses the need for the believer to **produce fruit after salvation**.

- **Second**, the contrast between Paul and James is **perspective**. Paul looks at life from **God's perspective** while James looks at life from a **human perspective**.
- **Third** is the contrast of **difference in terms**. Both Paul and James use the same word, *justified,* but with two different meanings.
  - By **justification**, Paul means the act of God at salvation whereby he declares the believing sinner **righteous** while still in a sinning state.
  - James uses the same word to mean "validation or evidence." We justify or prove our faith by our works, says James.

Expositional Study

To introduce the cardinal passage of this letter, James asks two rhetorical questions that beg for an answer and an analysis.

- What use is it if a person says he has faith, but has no works? (2:14). After pointing out the worthlessness of a workless faith, James then asks an even deeper question:
- Can such faith save him? (v.14). The answer is **NO!** Genuine, saving faith is accompanied by fruit.

Characteristics of Genuine Faith

James illustrates four marks of genuine faith (vv. 15–20).

- It is not indifferent ... but involved.
- Genuine faith is not independent ... but in partnership.
- Genuine faith is not invisible ... but on display.
- Genuine faith is not intellectual ... but from the heart.

Now we look at some **Examples of Genuine Faith** to emphasize this point. James now directs our attention to Abraham and Rahab (vv. 21–25).

James couldn't have chosen two more **contrasting** people as proof that our works prove our faith.

- Abraham was father of the Jews. Abraham was moral, admired, a Jewish patriarch.
- Rahab was a pagan prostitute. Rahab was a harlot, considered insignificant.

Yet both evidenced the same kind of faith! (Genesis 22 and Joshua 2).

Concluding Principle

James summarizes his entire discussions in verse 26.

When there is separation, there is death—both in the physical and the spiritual realms. Yes, faith, like calories, cannot be seen, but James says that you can always see its results.

Reflections

Genuine faith is involved ... is yours?
Genuine faith is partnership ... is yours?
Genuine faith is displayed ... is yours?
Genuine faith is from the heart ... is yours?

Bibliography

Allan, Frank. "Cheating At Church," in Barbara Brown Taylor, ed., *Ministry and Mission* (Atlanta: Post Horn, 1985)

Ackerman, John. *Listening to God: Spiritual Formation in Congregation* (Bethesda: The Alban Institute, 2001)

Allchin, A.M. "Anglican Spirituality." In *The Study of Anglicanism*. John Booty and Jonathan Knights, eds. (New York: Fortress Press, 1998)

Bailey, Boyd. *Learning to Lead like Jesus: 11 Principles to Help You Serve, Inspire & Equip Others* (Eugene, OR: Harvest House Publishers, 2018)

Bakke, Jeanette A. *Holy Invitations: Exploring Spiritual Direction* (Grand Rapids: Baker Books, 2000)

Barth Karl. *The Holy Spirit and the Christian Life* (Louisville: John Knox Press, 1993)

Benson, Robert. *A Good Life: Benedict's Guide to Everyday Joy* (Brewster, MA: Paraclete Press, 2004)

Bourgeault, Cynthia. *The Heart of Centering Prayer: Nondual Christianity in Theory and Practice* (Boulder, CO: Shambhala Publications, 2016)

Brown, Patricia D. *Paths to Prayer: Finding Your Own Ways to the Presence of God* (San Francisco: Jossey-Bass, 2003)

Brungs, Robert A. *A Priestly People* (New York: Sheed and Wand, 1968)

Carr, Wesley. *The Priestlike Task* (London: SPCK, 1985)

Casey, Michael. *Sacred Reading: The Art of Lectio Divina* (Liguori: Liguori Triumph, 1995)

Chan, Simon. *Spiritual Theology: A Systemic Study of Christian Life* (Downers Grove, IL: InterVarsity Press, 1998)

Chittister, Joan, OSB. *Wisdom Distilled from the Daily: Living the Rule of St. Benedict Today* (San Francisco: HarperCollins, 1991)

Croft, Stephen, ed. *Mission-Shaped Questions: Defining Issues for Today's Church* (London: Church House Publishing, 2008)

Chrysostom, John, quoted by Oliver Clements. *The Roots of Christian Mysticism* (New York: New City Press, 1995)

Chrysostom, St. John, tr. Henry Davis. "Six Books on the Priesthood" (Crestwood: St. Vladimir's Seminary Press, 1977)

Coleman, Roger, ed. *Resolution of the Twelve Lambeth Conferences: 1867–1988* (Toronto: Anglican Book Centre, 1992)

Coriden, James A. *An Introduction to Canon Law* (New York/ Mahwah: Paulist Press, 1991)

Countryman, L. William. *Living on the Border of the Holy: Renewing the Priesthood of All* (Harrisburg: Morehouse Publishing, 1999)

Chilcote, Paul W., and Laceye C. Warner, eds. *The Study of Evangelism: Exploring a Missional Practice of the Church* (Grand Rapids: William B. Eerdmans, 2008)

Davis, Kortright. *Serving with Power: Reviving the Spirit of Christian Ministry* (New York/Mahwah: Paulist Press, 1999)

Doe, Norman. *The Legal Framework of the Church of England: A Critical Study in a Comparative Context* (Oxford: Clarendon Press, 1998)

Ferlo, Roger. *Sensing God: Reading the Scriptures with All Our Senses* (Cambridge: Cowley Publications, 2002)

Foster, Richard J. *Celebration of Discipline: The Path to Spiritual Growth* (New York: HarperCollins, 1998)

Foster, Richard, with Kathryn A. Helmers. *Life with God: A Life-Transforming New Approach to Bible Reading* (London: Hodder & Stoughton, 2008)

Fretheim, Terrence E., and Karl Fried Froehlich. *The Bible as Word of God in a Postmodern Age* (Minneapolis: Fortress Press, 1998)

Fry, Timothy, OSB, ed. "The Rule of St. Benedict" (Collegeville: The Liturgical Press, 1982)

Garrett, Greg. *My Church is Not Dying: Episcopalians in the 21st Century* (New York: Morehouse Publishing, 2015)

Green, Thomas, SJ. *Prayer and Common Sense* (Notre Dame: Ave Maria Press, 1995)

Groeschel, Benedict J. *Spiritual Passages: The Psychology of Spiritual Development* (New York: Crossroad, 1988)

Gillquist, Peter E. *Designed for Holiness: God's Plan to Shape and Use You for His Kingdom* (Ann Arbor: Servant Books, 1986)

Holmes, Urban III. *Spirituality for Ministry* (Harrisburg: Morehouse Publishing, 2002)

Holmes, Urban T. III. *What Is Anglicanism?* (Harrisburg: Morehouse Publishing, 1982)

Hope, Susan. *Mission-Shaped Spirituality: Transforming Power of Mission* (London: Church House Publishing, 2006)

Hume, Basil, OSB. *The Intentional Life: The Making of a Spiritual Vocation* (Brewster, MA: Paraclete Press, 1977)

Kafwanka, John, and Mark Oxbrow, eds. *Intentional Discipleship and Disciple-Making* (London: The Anglican Consultative Council, 2016)

Keating, Thomas M., Basil Rennington, and Thomas Clarke. "Finding Grace at the Center" in *Old Wine in New Skins: Centering Prayer and Systems Theory*, ed. Paul David Lawson (New York: Lantern Books, 2001)

Kinast, Robert L. *Caring for Society: A Theological Interpretation of Lay Ministry* (Chicago: The Thomas More Press, 1985)

Leech, Kenneth. *True Prayer: An Introduction to Christian Spirituality* (London: Sheldon Press, 1980)

———. *Soul Friend: An Invitation to Spiritual Direction* (New York: HarperCollins Publishers, 1992)

———. *Spirituality and Pastoral Care* (Cambridge: Cowley Publications, 1989)

Lemler, James. *Transforming Congregations* (New York: Church Publishing, 2008)

John Paul II. *A Catechesis on the Creed – The Spirit: Giver of Life and Love*, Vol III (Boston: Pauline Books and Media, 1996)

———. *The Vocation and the Mission of the Lay Faithful in the Church and in the World: Christifideles Laici*, Post-Synodal Apostolic Exhortation (Washington: United States Catholic Conference, 1988)

Jones, Cheslyn, Geoffrey Wainwright, and Edward Yarnold, eds. *The Study of Spirituality* (New York: Oxford, 1986)

MacArthur, John. *Called to Lead: Leadership Lessons from the Life of the Apostle Paul* (Nashville: Thomas Nelson, 2004)

Macquarrie, John. *Principles of Christian Theology* (London: SCM Press, 1977)

Marshall, Michael E. *The Anglican Church Today and Tomorrow* (Wilton: Morehouse Publishing, 1982)

McAdoo, R. Henry, and Kenneth Stevenson. *The Mystery of the Eucharist in the Anglican Tradition* (Norwich: Canterbury Press, 1997)

McGrath, Alister E. *Christian Spirituality: An Introduction* (Oxford: Blackwell Publishing, 2003)

Merton, Thomas. *New Seeds of Contemplation* (New York: New Directions, 1961)

Middleton, Richard J., and Brian J. Walsh. *Truth Is Stranger than It Used to Be: Biblical Faith in a Postmodern Age* (Downers Grove, IL: InterVarsity, 1995)

Myers, Benjamin. *Christ the Stranger: A Theology of Rowan Williams* (New York: T&T Clark International, 2012)

Nemeck, Francis, and Marie Coombs. *The Spiritual Journey* (Collegeville: Liturgical Press, 1986)

Norgren, William A., ed. *Ecumenism of the Possible: Witness, Theology and the Future Church*. The Riverdale Report: Presentations and Documents of the National Consultation on Ecclesiology (Cincinnati: Forward Movement Publications, 1994)

Nouwen, Henri. *Creative Ministry* (New York: Image Books Doubleday, 1971)

————. *Reaching Out: The Three Movements of the Spiritual Life* (New York: Image Books Doubleday, 1975)

————. *The Wounded Healer* (New York: Image Books Doubleday, 1979)

O'Meara, Thomas Franklin. *Theology of Ministry* (New York/ Ramsey: Paulist Press, 1983)

Osborne, Keenan, BOFM. *Ministry: Lay Ministry in the Roman Catholic Church: Its History and Theology* (New York: Paulist Press, 1993)

Payne, Claude E. *Reclaiming Christianity: A Practical Model for Spiritual Growth and Evangelism* (Cincinnati: Forward Movement, 2018)

Peterson, Eugene. *The Contemplative Pastor: Returning to the Art of Spiritual Direction* (Grand Rapids: William Eerdmans Publishing, 1989)

Pittenger, Norman. The Ministry of All Christians: A Theology of Lay Ministry (Wilton: Morehouse-Barlow Co., 1983)

Pritchard, John. *The Life and Work of a Priest* (London: SPCK, 2007)

Radcliffe, Timothy, OP. *What is the Point of Being a Christian?* (London: Burns & Oates, 2008)

Robinson, Anthony B. and Robert W. Wall. *Called to Lead: Paul's Letters to Timothy for a New Day* (Grand Rapids: William B. Eerdmans, 2012)

Rohr, Richard. *Falling Upward: A Spirituality of Two Halves of Life* (London: Society for Promoting Christian Knowledge, 2012)

———. *Immortal Diamond: The Search for Our True Self* (London: Society for Promoting Christian Knowledge, 2013)

———. *Quest for the Grail* (New York: The Crossroad Publishing Co., 1994)

Rosenthal, James M., and Nicola Currie. *Being Anglican in the Third Millennium*, Anglican Consultative Council, Tenth Meeting, Panama City, Panama, 1996 (Harrisburg: Morehouse, 1996)

Stancliffe, David. "Baptism and Fonts" (*Ecclesiastical Law Journal* 3, no. 14, 1993)

Stevens, R. Paul. *The Other Six Days: Vocation, Work, and Ministry in Biblical Perspective* (Vancouver: Regent College Publishing, 1999)

St. Gregory the Great, tr. Graham Neville. "Pastoral Care" (Westminster: The Newman Press, 1950)

The Book of Common Prayer and Administration of the Sacraments and Other Rites and Ceremonies of the Church According to the Use of the Protestant Episcopal Church in the United States of America Together with Psalter, or Psalms of David (New York: Church Publishing Incorporated, 1979)

The Church in the Province of the West Indies: The Book of Common Prayer (1995)

Warren, Michael. *Faith, Culture and the Worshipping Community* (New York: Paulist Press, 1989)

Washburn, Michael. *Transpersonal Psychoanalytic Perspective* (Albany: State University of New York, 1994)

Wells, Samuel. *A Nazareth Manifesto: Being with God* (West Sussex: John Wiley, 2015)

Williams, Rowan. *Being Christian: Baptism, Bible, Eucharist, Prayer* (Grand Rapids: William B. Eerdmans, 2014)

———. *Faith in the Public Square* (London: Bloomsbury Publishing, 2012)

About the Author

At present, the author serves as the eleventh Episcopal Bishop of the Diocese of Easton and the Eastern Shore of Maryland, USA. Prior to this position he was parish priest in Guyana, South America (1981–1989), Bahamas (1989–2003), and Jacksonville, Florida (2003–2005). Later he was elected and served as the third Bishop of Seychelles, Province of the Indian Ocean (2005–2008); Assisting Bishop, Episcopal Diocese of East Carolina (2009–2012); and Assistant Bishop, Episcopal Diocese of Alabama (2012–2016).

In the global Anglican Communion, he served from 2006 to 2009 on the Anglican Communion Covenant Design Group and was subsequently appointed Commissary of the Archbishop of Canterbury, The Most Reverend Rowan William (2009–2012), to the global Anglican Communion, as a member the archbishop's Pastoral Visitors' Team. Membership of that body included the Most Reverend Justin Welby, during his time as Dean of Liverpool and Bishop of Durham. Archbishop Welby holds the highest office in the global Anglican Communion as the 105th Archbishop of Canterbury.

The author is a convert to Christianity from Hinduism, which was the religion of his parents and forebears, a faith which to some extent would have had some influence on his early upbringing. He was the first from the Caribbean of Asian (East) Indian origin to be elected bishop in the world wide Anglican Communion. With his election to the See of the Diocese of Easton, which covers the

Eastern shore of Maryland, he became the first Asian (East) Indian to be elected bishop in the Eastern and Western Hemispheres, and first person of color elected bishop in the over 150 year history of the diocese.

He grew up in a small village in rural Guyana, a village populated by predominantly Hindus, Muslims and few Christians that mainly attended St. Agnes Anglican Church. His early years, ten to twenty-three, were involved in rice farming. His summer breaks from seminary were spent in the rice fields. Rice farming in most third world developing countries is a very primitive operation, for all intents and purposes physically grueling and emotionally demanding. He credits much of his pastoral care qualities to his formation as a rice farmer. A discipline that required hard work, gentle care, patience, endurance, perseverance, commitment, long hours of waiting and watching, significant amount of prayer for a fruitful harvest, and the courage, determination and fortitude to continue even after you may have had a terrible season.

He holds a Diploma in Pastoral Studies from Codrington Theological College, Barbados; Bachelor of Arts in Theology, University of the West Indies, Barbados; Master in Sacred Theology in Christian Spirituality, General Theological Seminary, New York; Master of Law in Canon Law, University of Wales, Cardiff, United Kingdom; Doctor of Ministry, Colgate Rochester Divinity School/Bexley Hall Seminary, Rochester, New York; and Doctor of Divinity (Honoris Causa) from Bexley Hall Seminary and General Theological Seminary.

Printed in the United States
By Bookmasters